THE HOLOCAUST

100 Questions and Answers

Thomas Dalton

THE HOLOCAUST

100 Questions and Answers

Thomas Dalton

Clemens & Blair, LLC

— 2025 —

CLEMENS & BLAIR, LLC

Clemens & Blair, LLC, is a non-profit educational publisher.
www.clemensandblair.com

Library of Congress Cataloging-in-Publication Data

Dalton, Thomas
The Holocaust: 100 Questions and Answers

p. cm.
Includes bibliographical references

ISBN 978-1963-1431-57
(pbk.: alk. paper)

1. Holocaust, the
2. Jewish Question, the
3. History of Jews in Germany

Printing number: 9 8 7 6 5 4 3 2 1

Printed in the United States of America on acid-free paper.

ACKNOWLEDGMENT

The editor would like to acknowledge D. G., both for his inspiration for the present volume and for his material support that made this work possible.

CONTENTS

PREFACE

The purpose of this small book is to address some tough and pointed questions about the Holocaust. Much of what people know about this event is superficial, unexamined, and subject to a highly biased intention —namely, to promote an image of long-suffering Jews who are in constant need of aid and protection. A further purpose is to remind people— mostly White Europeans—that it was "they" (their people) who committed this atrocity and therefore that they must forever atone for it. The basic facts of this event, we are told, are etched in stone, never to be questioned or reexamined. Hence, objective and impartial analysis is almost completely lacking, especially in academia and the mass media. This leaves the thinking reader with a long list of basic questions; such questions are typically either ignored, censored, banned, or given wholly unsatisfactory replies.

The intent of the present book is to remedy this situation. Here, we offer a list of essential questions about the Holocaust and provide answers from all perspectives, including the traditional, orthodox view and from the more skeptical and critical 'revisionist' view. While it is not our intention here to promote one side or the other, we must acknowledge that one side—the conventional view—is utterly dominant in Western society today, whereas alternative, revisionist views are utterly suppressed, ignored, or censored. As a result, the revisionist case requires greater elaboration. That said, we offer here the views of all sides, provide some elementary analysis, and let the reader make up his own mind.

This booklet was inspired by a similar work, *The Holocaust: 120 Questions and Answers*, that was published back in 1983 by an early skeptic, Dr. Charles Weber. While useful in its day, Weber's questions and answers are frequently dated and, in some cases, incorrect. But we found the format of his book helpful and inspiring. Thus, we have undertaken this effort to revise both questions and answers in light of new information on the Holocaust that has appeared in the intervening 40+ years.

All the data, statistics, and quotations offered here have well-documented sources, and these are included in the Notes and References section at the end of the book; note-numbers correspond to the question of the same number. Also included at the end is a bibliography of most of the cited works; this also includes other works of general interest. Finally, we include a basic index of names and key terms.

In the end, it is our hope that this small book will shed some badly-needed light on one of the most consequential events of the 20th century: the Jewish Holocaust.

THE HOLOCAUST

100 Questions and Answers

PART 1
BASIC TERMS AND CONCEPTS

1. What is a "holocaust"?

The word 'holocaust' derives from the ancient Jewish word *olah*, meaning 'that which is completely burned.' It was common practice for ancient Jews to completely burn animals as a sacrifice to their god Yahweh (Jehovah); *olah* occurs nearly 300 times in the Old Testament. From roughly 1000 BC to the year 70 AD, Jews burned an estimated 45 animals per day—around two per hour, day and night, year-round—in their central temple in Jerusalem. (That temple was destroyed by the Romans in the year 70, and the sacrifices ceased.)

In 310 BC, Greek philosopher Theophrastus wrote about this Jewish practice, using the Greek word *holokautountes*, deriving from 'complete' (*holos*) 'burning' (*kaustos*). This became our English word 'holocaust,' which came into circulation around the year 1200 AD.

2. What was the "Jewish Holocaust"?

English-speaking Jews have used the word 'holocaust' for well over 100 years to refer to any kind of attack or mass tragedy of Jewish people. For example, the *New York Times* reported in 1903 on the Kishinev "massacre" in Russia in which some 80 Jews were killed; the initial report quotes the *Jewish Chronicle*: "We say [Russia] is steeped to the eyes in the guilt of this holocaust" (16 May, p. 1). Four days later, the paper quotes American Jew Oscar Straus, referring to the event as "this barbaric holocaust" (20 May, p. 2). Years later, in 1916, amidst World War One, the *Times* reported on concerns about Jews in the war zone "who have fallen under the blight of the world holocaust" (29 Oct, p. E9).

The word was first applied to Hitler's Germany at least by 1939, well before any alleged systematic killing occurred. The *Times* reports on one Rabbi Newman, who condemned "the holocaust of catastrophe which Hitler has visited on whole nations and masses of individuals" (24 Dec, p. 10). As a reference to 6 million Jewish victims, the first occurrence seems to have been in an August 1945 speech by Rabbi Chaim Weizmann, who referred to "so fearful a holocaust" in which "the Jews lost 6,000,000 victims to Nazism" (2 Aug, p. 11). By the early 1950s, this would evolve into reference to "the" Holocaust (with a capital 'H').

Today, the Holocaust refers specifically to the alleged murder of around 6 million Jews in Hitler's Germany by use of several methods, including mass shootings and alleged mass gassings in specially-built homicidal gas chambers. Hence, the Holocaust concept today has three central pillars: (1) intentionality on the part of the Germans; (2) use of homicidal gas chambers; and (3) some 6 million victims. Lacking any one of these three, we technically have no Holocaust. A tragedy, perhaps, but no Holocaust.

The conventional or orthodox Holocaust view, in which Hitler allegedly had genocidal intentions against the Jews, might be called the *Extermination Thesis*. This view has serious flaws, as we will see.

3. What is the view of Holocaust revisionists?

A revisionist is anyone who argues for a significant change or revision to the standard account of some historical event. Holocaust revisionists generally believe that (a) neither Hitler nor any of the leading Germans desired, or planned, the mass murder of the Jews; (b) there were no homicidal mass-gassing chambers in any camp; and (c) the number of Jews who died during the war was far less than 6 million—and perhaps as low as 500,000. Such revisionists therefore argue against not one, but all three of the main pillars of the Holocaust story.

It is also important to say what revisionists do *not* believe. They do not believe that "nothing happened" to the Jews. They do not believe that the Germans were innocent of all crimes. They do not deny that many Jews suffered and died under German rule. They do not deny that Hitler and leading Germans strongly disliked the Jews and wanted them removed from German society. They do not deny that many hundreds of thousands of Jews were starved, shot, or otherwise killed.

Therefore, the revisionists argue against the Extermination Thesis with a different view: what might be called the *Deportation Thesis*, in which Jews were forcibly rounded up, placed in temporary camps and detention facilities, and then systematically shipped to territories in the far east of Europe. Late in the war, many of these detained Jews were used for slave labor on behalf of the German war effort. But the long-term plan was always to eventually deport them from German territory.

4. So, was the Holocaust a hoax?

That depends on what we mean by 'hoax.' A hoax is generally a deliberate deception by someone for the purpose of personal gain; in other words, an intentional lie by someone who knew the truth. By this definition, the Holocaust would be a hoax only if someone—a governmental or civic leader, or top academic—knew that the Germans had no homicidal intention, or had no gas chambers, or that less than a million Jews died, but deliberately stated otherwise. Now, it is highly unlikely that anyone in 1946 or 1947 could have known the truth about such things and then deliberately stated otherwise, simply in order to create a myth of Jewish suffering. Therefore, it is unlikely that the Holocaust was originally a hoax.

However, if we accept a looser definition in which a hoax is an untruth promoted by someone who did, or should have, known better, then we might be able to justify such a label. Later Holocaust specialists like Gerald Reitlinger, Raul Hilberg, or Lucy Dawidowicz, not to mention current scholars like Deborah Lipstadt, Robert van Pelt, Ian Kershaw, Robert Evans, or Peter Longerich, clearly *did know,* or *should have known*, that much of the story was false, and therefore they might plausibly be called hoaxers. We cannot be sure what exactly they know, so it is hard to say for sure; but given the many problems with the orthodox account, we can be certain that either they are lying to us (if they know) or that they are grossly incompetent (if they do not know). Either way, it looks very bad for them.

5. Who are the major Holocaust revisionists?

Revisionism has existed since the very end of WW2, but it did not take on a serious academic quality until the 1960s with such men as Paul Rassinier and David Hoggan, and then in the 1970s with the work of Richard Verall (aka Harwood), Udo Walendy, Wilhelm Staeglich, and especially two professors: Robert Faurisson and Arthur Butz. Butz published his ground-breaking *The Hoax of the 20th Century* in 1976, which marked the beginning of serious, 'scientific' revisionism.

Academic revisionism accelerated in the 1980s and 1990s, based on research by Fred Leuchter, Germar Rudolf, Friedrich Berg, Juergen Graf, and Carlo Mattogno, among others. Especially from 2000 onward, the movement has been extremely productive; the current Holocaust Handbook series has over 50 volumes, on all aspects of the Holocaust. Notable revisionist works have been published by Thomas Kues, Samuel Crow-ell, Nick Kollerstrom, and Thomas Dalton. But chief credit must go to Rudolf and Mattogno; Rudolf's *Dissecting the Holocaust* and *Lectures on the Holocaust* are classic works in the field, and Mattogno's 25+ volumes represent a monumental research and documentation effort that will surely never be matched. And the recent revisionist *Holocaust Encyclopedia* is yet another major milestone in advancing a general awareness of the issues at hand.

In sum, revisionists can now say with confidence that virtually every significant aspect of the orthodox Holocaust has been undermined. In particular, the three pillars—intentionality, gas chambers, and 6 million Jewish fatalities—have been all but demolished. Vast revisionist documentation shows that Hitler and his officers sought only to remove Jews from the Reich; that homicidal gas chambers cannot have functioned in the manner claimed; and that far less than 6 million Jews died.

6. Why haven't we heard about these revisionists and their work?

It is highly revealing to see how orthodox researchers respond to revisionist achievements. First, most mainstream researchers ignore or actively censor revisionist work. Only a very few—notably, Deborah Lipstadt and Richard Evans—have elected to respond. But their responses are highly biased and tendentious, if not to say incompetent. They resort to name-calling (revisionists are "Holocaust deniers") and slander (revisionists are malicious, evil, neo-Nazis). They cite only the oldest and least-relevant—and often deceased—revisionists while completely ignoring the recent, high-quality work by Mattogno, Rudolf, Graf, and others. Indeed, it is almost impossible to find specific reference to such men in any orthodox account of the Holocaust; such is the degree of fear and cowardice.

Further, academia and mass media do nothing to advance an honest discussion of the issues, and instead take all action to censor, disparage, or ignore revisionist work. Dalton's *Debating the Holocaust* demonstrates the sorry state of affairs by showing the strength of revisionist claims and the inadequacy of orthodox replies. Beyond this, governments around the world have actually *outlawed* revisionist work and writing; they are clearly terrified that revisionist arguments will hold sway and bring a highly uncomfortable truth to light. This occurs because many figures in Western governments are themselves Jews or are financially beholden to Jewish money, and thus defend the present account, which sustains the notion of an innocent but beleaguered Jewish people who are perpetually in need of financial, political, and military assistance.

It is clear that, on all counts, those in positions of power prefer to sustain the current but false view of the Holocaust. They have no incentive to discuss or examine revisionist claims, and so they resort to censorship and legal prohibitions to block all such ideas from reaching the public sphere. They have no interest in the truth; they much prefer a false and distorted version of history, and are more than happy to promote such a falsehood in schools, universities, motion pictures, and popular culture. The overall situation is highly damning for the credibility of Western governments, media, and academia.

7. How do Jews benefit from the orthodox Extermination Thesis?

For centuries, Jews have fostered an image of themselves as a perpetually abused and oppressed people, always at the hands of evil anti-Semites. This image goes back to the days of the Babylonian Captivity (around 600 BC) and includes the Roman Empire, the Inquisition, various exiles and banishments of Jews from Europe in the Middle Ages, Russian pogroms, and the 'Nazi' persecution of the 20th century. In this fairytale image, the innocent Jews are constantly in need of aid and assistance, and of special protections, lest any anti-Semitic ruler or nation attack them again. But they themselves are always guilt-free and never do anything wrong or objectionable—or so the story goes.

The Holocaust, though, was "uniquely evil" in that Hitler allegedly wanted to physically murder every Jew in Europe—and that he allegedly succeeded in killing 6 million of them in the most horrendous ways, including gas chambers. Hence, Jews claim that their people were the primary victims of WW2 (in which some 60 million people died overall), and therefore that they are deserving of special protections and reparations, both now and in the future, for all time.

The first benefit for them was a decision by the UN in late 1947 to create a new state of Israel, which would become effective in May of 1948. Zionist Jews had been working for this goal since the 1600s, but only with the coming of WW2, and in light of the "exterminationist" Holocaust, did the UN agree to grant their demand.

Secondly, at the Versailles Peace Conference after WWI, Jewish delegates from the US and all nations achieved virtually all of their aims: increased political power in the victor-nations, financial reparations, "anti-anti-Semitism" legislation, punishment of their enemies, and so on.

Third is the guilt-complex thrust upon Germans, Europeans, Americans, and indeed all Whites everywhere: Whites either perpetrated or failed to stop crimes against the Jews, and thus they are all complicit. Consequently, even today, many Whites feel compelled to cede to any and all Jewish demands, no matter how unjustified or outrageous.

Fourth, the global Jewish Lobby uses the Holocaust to seize a high moral ground on all issues, thus aiding their ongoing quest for wealth, power, and privilege. All actions by Jews or Israel, even the most criminal ones, are deemed justified and permissible, owing to the special moral status conferred on Jews by the Holocaust.

Fifth is financial reparations, paid by Germany and other nations, to Israel and various Jewish agencies. To date, Germany has paid some $100 billion since the war. And not only Germany; Austria, Switzerland, Italy, Belgium, and other nations have been coerced to pay hundreds of millions in reparations. And even the US, which continues to provide at least $6 billion in foreign aid to Israel every year, can be seen as providing a kind of reparation.

In sum, Jews everywhere have profited immensely from the Holocaust. They have a huge interest in sustaining the existing orthodox account, and a corresponding interest in suppressing revisionist ideas. The success of revisionism could significantly reduce the wealth and power that they accrue, and it would undoubtedly crush their claimed high moral ground. It could even be their "Achilles' heel," serving as the keystone in completely dismantling Jewish power around the world. Therefore, Jews spare no expense in censoring, harassing, intimidating, suing, or legislating against revisionists.

PART 2
THE CONDITION OF EUROPEAN JEWS
BEFORE WORLD WAR TWO

8. Isn't it true that European Jews were oppressed for decades or even centuries prior to WW2?

For at least 2,000 years, Jews have been a powerful and influential minority. In the Roman Empire, in the year 59 BC, Cicero wrote about "how influential they [the Jews] are in informal assemblies," which strongly suggests the kind of "backroom dealing" for which Jews are famous today. In the year 60 AD, Seneca complained that "this accursed race" had become sufficiently powerful as to be "received throughout all the world."

Many centuries later, beginning with the French Revolution and continuing throughout the 1800s, Jews in Europe progressively gained civil rights and privileges, and were treated as fully equal citizens. In the process, they also gained substantial wealth and power, primarily through ethically dubious and exploitative lending practices. Jews also worked together in tightly-knit networks, serving each other's interests and skirting or flouting legal regulations. Through assorted strong-arm measures and other ruthless tactics, they came to dominate certain sectors of European society, including finance, press, theater, and vital commodities. For centuries, they were certainly the most powerful minority in Europe.

As early as 1798, German philosopher Immanuel Kant remarked that "the wealth of the Jews...apparently exceeds per capita that of any other nation at the present time." In 1823, the poet Lord Byron wrote "all states, all things, all sovereigns [the Jews] control." In 1843, Bruno Bauer observed that "the Jew...determines the fate of the whole [Austrian] Empire by his financial power. The Jew...decides the destiny of Europe."

By 1850, German composer Richard Wagner could complain that much of the music business had been 'Judaized' and hence debased, pandering to low tastes and placing profits over quality. Worse, much of European society was controlled by Jews. It was no longer a question of "emancipation" of the Jews but rather coming to grips with their power.

Wagner wrote: "According to the present constitution of the world, the Jew in truth is already more than emancipated; he *rules*, and will rule, so long as money remains the power before which all our doings and our dealings lose their force." Where money rules, Jews rule: this was his message. Hence, "Jewry itself is the evil conscience of our modern civilization."

In a follow-up essay of 1869, Wagner noted that the European press was "entirely directed by Jews"; control of the press, combined with their accumulated wealth, resulted in a Jewry that was "the mightiest organization of our time."

In 1873, writer Frederick Millingen published a booklet entitled *The Conquest of the World by the Jews*. There, he wrote that "the Jews…are now the wealthiest and most influential class of men; and [they] have attained a position of vast power, the likes of which we do not meet in all history."

Specifically with respect to Germany, in 1879, journalist Wilhelm Marr published an influential essay, *The Victory of Jewry over Germandom*, decrying the fact that "Jewry has triumphed on a worldwide historical basis." Into a naïve and innocent Germany "penetrated a smooth, crafty, pliable Jewry" that defeated "the monarchical, knightly, lumbering German by enabling him in his vices"—that is, by exploiting his weaknesses. "Germany is finished," concludes Marr.

Thus we see that, far from being "poor and oppressed," European Jews effectively ruled not only Europe but vast portions of the known world, for centuries. It was into such a world that Adolf Hitler was born, in 1889.

9. But the Jews were expelled many times over the centuries, were they not?

Yes, this is true—actually, hundreds of times over the past 3,000 years. The first major expulsion was by Babylonian king Nebuchadnezzar II in 597 BC, who captured Jerusalem and evacuated many Jews. Then were several expulsions by the Romans during the Roman Empire, including in 139 BC (expelled from Rome), 19 AD (again from Rome), 38 AD (from Alexandria), 50 AD (again from Rome), 70 AD (when Rome defeated the Jewish revolt in Jerusalem), in 117 (after the 2nd revolt), and in 135 AD (after the 3rd revolt).

In the Middle Ages, expulsions accelerated in Europe. The major events included:

- 1012 AD (from Mainz, Germany)
- 1182 (Paris)
- 1231 (Leicester, England)
- 1253 (Vienne, France)
- 1254 (all of France)
- 1276 (Bavaria)
- 1288 (Naples, Italy)
- 1290 (all of England)
- 1294 (Bern, Switzerland)

Into the Renaissance, troubles with Jews continued as before:

- 1306 (France again)
- 1322 (again)
- 1359 (again)
- 1360 (Hungary)
- 1392 (Bern again)
- 1394 (France again)
- 1421 (Vienna)
- 1442 (Bavaria again)
- 1478 (Passau, Germany)
- 1491 (Ravenna, Italy)
- 1492 (most of Spain)
- 1496 (Portugal)
- 1499 (Nuremberg, Germany)

Things were no better into the 16th century:

- 1510 (Naples again)
- 1515 (Dubrovnik)
- 1519 (Regensburg, Germany)
- 1526 (Bratislava)
- 1551 (Bavaria again)
- 1596 (all papal states)
- 1597 (Milan)
- 1614 (Frankfurt)
- 1670 (Vienna again)

Again, these were only the major events.

10. But why did this happen?
Yes: Why did this happen? Why so many expulsions, and why so many *repeated* expulsions from the same places? It cannot be due to simple-minded "anti-Semitism"; clearly the Jews were doing something objectionable, *very* objectionable, and doing it repeatedly, such as to create a popular uprising against them. Predatory lending, cheating at business, and general immorality and lawlessness are all certainly parts of the explanation.

But the core of the problem is rooted in the Jewish worldview. Even from biblical times, Jews have viewed themselves as better, greater, and more beloved of God ("chosen") than anyone else. They furthermore took this as a sign that they had a right, even a duty, to rule over others—*all* others, whom they viewed as lowly sub-humans. Thus, all the problems are grounded in (a) Jewish hatred of all non-Jewish people ("misanthropy") and (b) Jewish striving for "dominion" or world domination. We may combine these two characteristics under the heading of 'Jewish supremacism'—a situation that has not changed in thousands of years. This is why they have been hated for millennia.

Hitler and the Germans were obviously no aberration; they were only the latest in a very long line of governments to respond to popular demand and to expel their Jews. There was neither anything particularly unique or particularly evil about "Nazi Germany."

11. Doesn't this conflict with the point above, namely, that the Jews had wealth and power?

No. Oftentimes in history, the most powerful were the most hated by ordinary people, precisely because of their abuse of power. The Jews did have wealth and power all throughout the long period of expulsions, but not *enough* wealth or *enough* power to stop the sovereigns (kings, queens, popes, etc.) from driving them out. Only in the past 100 years or so have Jews had such obscene levels of wealth and power that they have been able to stifle all criticism, end all governmental 'oppression,' and to truly compel nations to follow their demands. Hitler was the last, best hope of the common people to drive out the pernicious Jewish element from Europe. But global Jewry was able to direct major nations against him and destroy him. Now we must live with the consequences.

12. Didn't the Russians persecute Jews in the late 1800s?

The Russians have long been troubled by their large Jewish population. By the late 1800s, the country had some 5 million Jews within its borders, mostly in the far western region called the Pale of Settlement; this represented about half of all Jews on Earth. They were a disruptive and agitating force within Russia and hence earned the dislike of Czars Nicholas I and Alexander II. Already in 1871, Russian activist Mikhail Bakunin remarked caustically that "this whole Jewish world…constitutes a single exploiting sect, a sort of bloodsucker people, a collective parasite…"

In 1881, a partly-Jewish anarchist gang succeeded in assassinating Alexander II, unleashing a series of anti-Jewish actions that persisted for decades. Naturally, from the Jewish perspective, this was a terrible tragedy, a catastrophe, even, yes, a "holocaust"—the first in modern history. And the number of Jews under assault—five to (later) six million—became an iconic figure.

13. Wait—so, there were reports of "6 million suffering Jews" already back in the 1800s?

By 1891, the *New York Times* began reporting on Jewish suffering in Russia; remarkably, their reports often included reference to a figure of "6 million." In 1891, we read about the sorry state of "Russia's population of 5,000,000 to 6,000,000 Jews," and of "the fact that about six millions persecuted and miserable wretches" still cling to their religion, against all odds. A few years later, and referring to the Russian Jews, Jewish activist Stephen Wise was quoted in the NYT as saying "There are 6,000,000 living, bleeding, suffering arguments in favor of Zionism" (11 June 1900, p. 7). In 1901, the *Chicago Daily Tribune* reported on the "hopeless condition" of the "six million Jews in Russia" (22 Dec, p. 13).

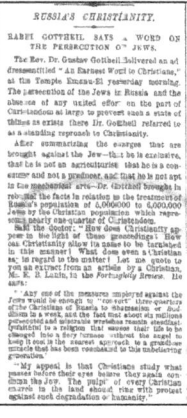

A minor pogrom occurred in the Russian city of Kishinev in 1903; the NYT dubbed this "a massacre," and reported a statement by the *Jewish Chronicle*: "We say it [the Russian government] is steeped to the eyes in the guilt of this holocaust. ... [The Jews are seen as] a perilous pest which must be slowly annihilated, [and Russians] will think themselves justified in accelerating the process of extermination..." (16 May, p. 1). This Russian "holocaust" was thus, amazingly, a precursor to much of the same talk about Germany in the 1940s.

Periodic and often minor anti-Jewish actions were always portrayed in the most dramatic terms. The NYT despaired over "our 6,000,000 cringing brothers in Russia" (23 Mar 1905, p. 7). Later that year came a polemic against a Russian leader who "caused 6,000,000 Jewish families to be expelled" (1 Nov, p. 2)—which is impossible, incidentally, since that would have involved some 25 million Jews. In 1906, we read of "startling reports of the condition and future of Russia's 6,000,000 Jews"; it is a "horrifying picture" of "renewed massacres" and "systematic and murderous extermination" (25 Mar, p. SM6). Suffice it to say that no concrete evidence of such massacres has ever surfaced.

Dr. Paul Nathan's View of Russian Massacre

STARTLING reports of the condition and future of Russia's 6,000,000 Jews were made on March 12 in Berlin to the annual meeting of the Central Jewish Relief League of Germany by Dr. Paul Nathan, a well-known Berlin publicist, who has returned from an extensive trip through Russia as the special emissary of Jewish philanthropists in England, America, and Germany, to arrange for distribution of the relief fund of $1,500,000 raised after the massacres last Autumn.

Dr. Nathan paints a horrifying picture of the plight and prospects of his coreligionists, and forecasts at any hour renewed massacres exceeding in extent and terror all that have gone before. He left St. Petersburg with the firm conviction that the Russian Government's studied policy for the "solution" of the Jewish question is systematic and murderous extermination.

In 1910, we find "Russian Jews in sad plight," and we are saddened over "the systematic, relentless, quiet grinding down of a people of more than 6,000,000 souls" (11 Apr, p. 18). In 1911, the NYT reported that "the 6,000,000 Jews of Russia are singled out for systematic oppression and for persecution by due process of law" (31 Oct, p. 5). Once again, we find '6 million'; 'systematic'; 'extermination'—another clear anticipation of things to come. And on 10 December, we read once more of "the oppression of the Jews, and by which [Russia] is making the 6,000,000 Jews a people economically exhausted—a people without any rights at all." (p. SM8) And all this *prior to World War One*.

14. What are the implications of this?
It means that all the key ideas—extermination, annihilation, "6 million," "holocaust"—were in place long before Hitler came to power. And, given that there is no evidence of more than a mere fraction of 6 million Jews having died, we see clear indication of massive exaggeration of Jewish suffering. The key elements of the Holocaust had already been deployed, falsely, against Russia in the early 1900s; thus, we can well understand that they might have again been used falsely against Hitler.

15. Weren't there again claims of massive Jewish suffering during WWI?
Indeed there were. Remarkably, the claims from the NYT and other Jewish media mirrored the claims from Russia just a few years earlier, using all the same language. Thus we can read in the NYT:

- "Appeal for aid for Jews: American Committee tells of Suffering Due to War. The American Jewish Relief Committee called a conference…to consider the plight of more than 6,000,000 Jews who live within the war zone." (2 Dec 1914)
- "In the world today there are about 13,000,000 Jews, of whom more than 6,000,000 are in the very heart of the war zone; Jews whose lives are at stake and who today are subjected to every manner of sorrow and suffering." (14 Jan 1915)
- The Russian government "has only one aim in view, to exterminate the Jewish race." (15 April 1915)
- The head of a Jewish aid society "declared that even the wrongs of the Belgians could not be compared to the outrages heaped upon the Polish Jews. 'Nearly six million Jews are ruined, in the

greatest moral and material misery... And the world is silent'." (28 Feb 1916)

- "Six millions of Jews are living in lands where they are oppressed, exploited, crushed, and robbed of every inalienable human right." (22 Jan 1917)
- An appeal for an aid fund "to alleviate the suffering of Jews in the European war zones... [whose] suffering is unparalleled in history. ... [W]omen, children, and babies must be saved if the Jewish race is to survive the terrible holocaust..." (24 Sep 1917)
- "6,000,000 Jews need Help." (18 Oct 1918)

JEWS' INDIFFERENCE TO WAR AID REBUKED

Louis Marshall Denounces Apathy Toward Suffering of Co-Religionists.

MILLIONS IN DIRE DISTRESS

Jacob H. Schiff, Meyer London, and Dr. Enelow Plead with the Rich to Give.

Louis Marshall, speaking at a meeting in Temple Emanu-El last night, deplored what he termed the failure of the Jews of America, particularly of New York, to realize the terrible calamity that has overtaken the millions of Jews whose homes are in the eastern theatre of the European war.

The meeting was held in the interest of the American Jewish Relief Committee, of which committee Mr. Marshall is President. Besides Mr. Marshall Congressman-elect Meyer London, and the Rev. Dr. H. G. Enelow of Temple Emanu-El spoke. Like Mr. Marshall, each deplored the fact that the Jews of America have not given the assistance they should to their suffering coreligionists. Further emphasis on the same subject was contained in a letter from Jacob H. Schiff, read by Mr. Marshall.

"It is discouraging," said Mr. Marshall," to those who have devoted so much time and energy to this work that there has been so small a response from Jews in New York, a city which is so great a Jewish centre. It seems to me that the people are so dazed by the European cataclysm that they are unable to realize that it is their duty to aid of those who are suffering through the calamity.

"In the world today there are about 13,000,000 Jews, of whom more than 6,000,000 are in the very heart of the war zone; Jews whose lives are at stake and who today are subjected to every manner of suffering and sorrow, and the great American Jewish community is not doing its duty toward these sufferers. In the United States there are between 2,000,000 and 3,000,000 Jews, nearly all able to do something and yet, after months of work, we have not raised more than $300,000. In New York there are more than 1,000,000 Jews, some of them persons of great affluence, but many of them seem to think if they give a few hundred dollars they have done their duty.

ASSAILS JEWISH RACE IDEA.

Rabbi Schulman Says Religion Alone Should Mark His People.

A warning that the enthronement of race consciousness among the Jews would result disastrously for them was uttered yesterday by Rabbi Samuel Schulman in a sermon on " The Jew's Business," at Temple Beth-El.

Dr. Schulman held that Jews were making a great mistake in indulging in the dominant thought of race and in an intensively exclusive nationalism. He maintained that to act thus was to shut out the larger view of the international brotherhood of men from the thought of the world. If once the idea of race permeates the thought of the Western World, he said, the position of the Jew would be worse than it had ever been in the history of this hemisphere. Continuing he said:

"We hear today very much of the rights of little nations. No voice is raised on behalf of Israel. Six millions of Jews are living in lands where they are oppressed, exploited, crushed, and robbed of every inalienable human right. The world does not recognize the Jews as an ordinary nation, in the sense in which it talks of the nationality of various peoples."

$1,000,000,000 FUND TO REBUILD JEWRY

Six Million Souls Will Need Help to Resume Normal Life When War Is Ended.

LOANS WITHOUT INTEREST

Committee of American Jews Lays Plans for the Greatest Humanitarian Task in History.

The American people, Jews and non-Jews alike, will soon be asked to lend or contribute the larger part of a fund of approximately $1,000,000,000 to carry out plans for the reconstruction of the Jewry of the entire world. Announcement to this effect, together with the general plan of procedure, was made public last night, following a meeting held yesterday in the office of Felix M. Warburg of Kuhn, Loeb & Co., Chairman of the Joint Distribution Committee of the American Funds for Jewish War Sufferers.

While the appeal will go out to the entire world, the people of war-ravaged Europe, it is believed, will not be in position to further the plan financially to any large extent, so that the burden will fall upon the United States, Canada, and perhaps England.

The money for the project, the largest purely humanitarian undertaking in history, will not be sought alone through contributions, but will embrace loans, and will be accepted from non-Jewish as well as Jewish sources. The exact date and the duration of the campaign for the billion-dollar reconstruction fund was not announced, but preliminary work has already begun.

The plan is the result of months of study by the Joint Distribution Committee of reports from every country in which Jews have been made to suffer through the war, and includes the sending of commissions of American Jews, experts in philanthropy, social service, education, and business, to Russia, Rumania, Poland, Palestine, Serbia, Greece, Bulgaria, and other lands as soon as the international situation permits. The work has already been initiated in several countries where recent allied successes have made a beginning possible.

6,000,000 Jews Need Help.

From reports from representatives abroad it is estimated that of the 9,000,000 to 12,000,000 souls making up the Jewish population of the world, exclusive of the 3,000,000 Jews in the United

And we must bear in mind that all this appeared in print during or immediately after WWI. That war was evidently a second Jewish "holocaust," complete with 6 million victims, following not long after the Russian one. And it set the stage for a *third* "holocaust," in Hitler's Germany. When it comes to the Jews, history indeed repeats itself.

16. What are the implications of this for the alleged Nazi Holocaust?
As twice before, we have extreme language used without evidence and without justification, simply to create an impression of massive Jewish suffering, in order to demand aid and assistance for the Jews. Once again, we have another strong piece of evidence that if this story was falsely used once against the Russians, and a second time during WWI, that we should not be surprised to see it recur a third time, also falsely, during WW2.

17. So, how many NYT references were there to "6 million" suffering Jews before WW2?
Literally dozens. Above we saw several examples, but the number continued to recur periodically after the First World War. In September of 1919, we find that it is now the *Ukrainian* and *Polish* Jews who are subject to misery: "6,000,000 are in peril" (8 Sep, p. 6). We are further horrified to read that "the population of 6,000,000 souls in Ukrainia and in Poland… are going to be completely exterminated."

By this time, other periodicals were playing up the infamous number. As an example, we have this notable piece from the journal *American Hebrew*:

> From across the sea six million men and women call to us for help, and eight hundred thousand little children cry for bread. … In this catastrophe, when six million human beings are being whirled toward the grave by a cruel and relentless fate… Six million men and women are dying from lack of the necessaries of life… In this threatened *holocaust* of human life… (31 Oct 1919, p. 582)

Thereafter followed a string of similar reports, all in the NYT:

- "unbelievable poverty, starvation and disease [for] about 6,000,000 souls, or half the Jewish population of the earth" (12 Nov 1919, p. 7).
- "typhus menaced 6,000,000 Jews of Europe" (12 Apr 1920, p. 16).
- "hunger, cold rags, desolation, disease, death—six million human beings without food, shelter, clothing" (2 May 1920, p. E1).
- A new fund "for Jewish war sufferers in Central and Eastern Europe, where six millions face horrifying conditions of famine, disease, and death" (7 May 1920, p 11).
- "Russia's 6,000,000 Jews are facing extermination by massacre"—again! (20 Jul 1921, p. 2).

JEWS ASK PUBLIC TO AID WAR VICTIMS

Non-Sectarian Appeal for $7,-500,000 Starts Today with Sermons in All Churches.

POLAND'S WOE APPALLING

Campaign to be Pressed by 10,000 Active Workers in the Five Boroughs.

A famished child upon the auction block, a mother in the foreground pleading for aid, death with outstretched arms lurking near and the legend, "Shall Death Be the Highest Bidder?"

Such is the pictorial representation of the needs of stricken peoples in the war-devastated zones of Central and Eastern Europe which will confront New York-ers everywhere today. Back of that representation stands an organization designed to take advantage of every channel to press home to the people of this city the need for contributing toward the $7,500,000 to be raised here this week for the Greater New York Appeal for Jewish War Sufferers.

This fund is but a tithe of that which must be subscribed in the entire country if disaster to whole peoples is to be averted. The world nature of the calamity which has overtaken men, women and children, deprived not only of life's bare necessities but of all means of rehabilitating themselves without aid from the outside, has led leading Jews of New York and the nation to turn to the public irrespective of creed, for help. Heretofore the Jews themselves have contributed many, many millions which have been expended by the Joint Distribution Committee through relief agencies of all countries and without regard to the religious beliefs of those in need. This time the burden is too gigantic to be borne by Jews alone.

Millions Racked by War.

A pen picture of actual conditions typical of those in several countries, has been sent to the Campaign Committee by Dr. Boris D. Bogen of this city, now in Warsaw as head of the First Relief Unit, sent abroad by the Joint Distribution Committee. Dr. Bogen writes:

"Hunger, cold rags, desolation, disease, death—Six million human beings without food, shelter, clothing or medical treatment in what now are but the wastes of once fair lands, lands ravaged by long years of war or blighted by its consequences!

"That, in a few words, is the actual situation in all those countries that constituted what was known during the great conflict as the Eastern theatre of war.

TELLS SAD PLIGHT OF JEWS.

Felix M. Warburg Says They Were the Worst Sufferers In War.

Felix M. Warburg, Chairman of the Joint Distribution Committee of American Funds for Jewish War Sufferers, who returned several days ago from a trip to Europe for that organization, made public yesterday some of his findings.

"The successive blows of contending armies have all but broken the back of European Jewry," he said, "and have reduced to tragically unbelievable poverty, starvation and disease about 6,000,-000 souls, or half the Jewish population of the earth.

"The Jewish people throughout Eastern Europe, by sheer accident of geography, have suffered more from the war than any other element of the population. The potential vitality and the capacity for self-help that remains to these people after the last five years is amazing to me."

pg 11

JEWISH WAR AID GETS $100,000 GIFT

Nathan Straus Tells Sympathy for Coreligionists in Europe.

DAY'S TOTAL IS $416,000

LaGuardia Promises Workers Aldermanic Committee to Help Drive.

The fund for Jewish war sufferers in Central and Eastern Europe, where six millions face horrifying conditions of famine, disease and death, was enriched yesterday by a contribution of $100,000 from Nathan Straus. Rabbi Stephen S. Wise announced the gift at yesterday afternoon's gathering in the Hotel Biltmore of workers seeking to raise New York's $7,500,000 quota of the $35,000,000 sought throughout the nation. The announcement brought the men and women there cheering to their feet.

"If American Jews now fail to help those who suffer through no fault of their own, Mr. Straus has said to me," Dr. Wise told the meeting. "the blame will rest upon their own heads should they miserably perish. Surely no self-respecting American Jew will wish, or even will suffer, the extinction of large numbers of Jewish people to come to

BEGS AMERICA SAVE 6,000,000 IN RUSSIA

Massacre Threatens All Jews as Soviet Power Wanes, Declares Kreinin, Coming Here for Aid.

Copyright, 1921, by The Chicago Tribune Co.

BERLIN, July 19.—Russia's 6,000,000 Jews are facing extermination by massacre. As the famine is spreading, the counter-revolutionary movement is gaining and the Soviet's control is waning. This statement is borne out by official documents presented to the Berlin Government, which show that numerous pogroms are raging in all parts of Russia and the Ukraine.

The information was gathered by Dr. Joseph Kreinin, a noted Jewish social worker and President of the Russian Joint Board of Jewish Societies. He says that several villages have been burned already and scores killed, seventy in one village alone. He is en route to America, where he plans meetings in New York, Chicago and elsewhere for the purpose of "saving his people."

According to Dr. Kreinin, mass flights from Russia have already begun, the Jews rushing to all borders and especially to Rumania, where there are 40,000 families camping along the frontier, hoping to find refuge. Among these, he says, at least 100 persons daily are dying from exposure and hunger.

Dr. Kreinin, who recently escaped from Moscow, says the pogroms are especially severe in the provinces of Homel, Minsk and Volhynia. The pogroms originated outside of Russia, in the Ukraine and White Russia.

For the next few years, the '6 million' fell into disuse, but it was reawakened when Hitler assumed power in January 1933. The NYT reported on a "Hitler protest" vote by some local New York government officials. Rabbi Stephen Wise issued an appeal: "We in America have taken the lead in a battle for the preservation of German Jewry," adding that his group "is now active in relief and reconstruction work in Eastern Europe where 6,000,000 Jews are involved" (29 Mar, p. 9). Thereafter, the number appears with growing frequency:

- We read in the *London Times* of "6,000,000 unwanted unfortunate" Jews, and of "these 6,000,000 people without a future" (26 Nov 1936, p. 15).

- On that same day, the NYT reported on a speech by British Zionist Chaim Weizmann, who "dwelt first on the tragedy of at least 6,000,000 'superfluous' Jews in Poland, Germany, Austria."
- In early 1937, we hear that "five to six million Jews in Europe are facing expulsion or direst poverty" (26 Feb, p. 12).
- In 1938, the NYT ran an article headlined "Persecuted Jews Seen on Increase" (9 Jan, p. 12). "6,000,000 victims noted," they said—referring to a combined total in Germany, Poland, and Romania.
- The very next month we hear about "a depressing picture of 6,000,000 Jews in Central Europe, deprived of protection or economic opportunities, slowly dying of starvation, all hope gone..." (23 Feb, p. 23).
- By May, it was the "rising tide of anti-Semitism in Europe today which has deprived more than 6,000,000 Jews and non-Aryans of a birthright" (2 May, p. 18).
- Later in 1938, the *London Times* printed an account of the "treatment of German Jews"; "the problem now involved some 6,000,000 Jews," they wrote (22 Nov, p. 11).
- Into early 1939, the *London Times* continued to report on Weizmann's view that "the fate of 6,000,000 people was in the balance" (14 Feb, p. 9).

PERSECUTED JEWS SEEN ON INCREASE

Dr. Kahn Returns With Report of Rise in Europe of Those Deprived of Rights

6,000,000 VICTIMS NOTED

25,000 Refugees Said to Be in Need—Rumania Menaces 800,000 With Anti-Semitism

The number of Jews deprived of their rights and economic opportunity in Europe increased greatly last year, Dr Bernhard Kahn, European director of the American Jewish Joint Distribution Committee, said on his arrival here last week from Europe.

The new Government of Rumania has threatened to outlaw 800,000 Rumanian Jews, "disregarding peace treaties, minority treaties and the constitution of the country," said Dr Kahn

NAZI PUBLICITY HERE HELD SMOKE SCREEN

Propaganda Called Cover to Destroy Democracy

The Nazi regime's attempts to conquer America by propaganda and anti-Semitism is only the smoke screen for its ultimate aims to destroy democratic institutions, it was said yesterday by Dr. Nahum Goldmann, chairman of the administrative committee of the World Jewish Congress, who arrived here last Friday from Switzerland.

"Six million Jews in Europe are doomed to destruction," Dr. Goldmann said in an interview at the Hotel Astor. "If the victory of the Nazis should be final. The only hope for them lies in a British victory."

He called upon American Jews to follow the example of the American people and urged them to create a united defense. He announced the formation of a Pan-American Jewish Congress for the protection of Jewish rights and said that this body, with the participation of Latin-American delegations would soon hold its first session in this country.

War began in September of that year, and anti-Nazi propaganda accelerated. In mid-1940, the NYT quoted Nahum Goldmann: "Six million Jews are doomed to destruction if the victory of the Nazis should be final" (25 Jun, p. 4). This was still at least *one full year* before Hitler allegedly decided to begin his program of Jewish mass murder—according to traditional experts. How could Goldmann have known what was to come?

18. What can we conclude from all these references?

This cannot be a coincidence: the repeated recurrence of the same number effectively proves that it is strictly symbolic: a stand-in for "many Jews" or "all of the Jews," but lacking any factual basis. (The number 6, in fact, seems to have some special meaning in Judaic numerology; just recall the infamous number '666' that appears in the Jewish-authored Book of Revelation.) In no case were 6 million Jews actually suffering, or actually dying. And the same was certainly true for the German Holocaust. The "6 million Jews" allegedly killed by Hitler is just a symbolic way of saying "Hitler killed lots of Jews"—which is true; but far fewer than 6 million, as we will see.

PART 3

THE RISE OF HITLER AND NATIONAL SOCIALISM

19. But Hitler did hate the Jews, right? Didn't he admit to being an anti-Semite?

Hitler did indeed hate the Jews and he did openly admit to being an anti-Semite. But the key point is what drove him to these opinions. No one is born anti-Semitic; there are very good reasons why people, for millennia, have come to dislike Jews.

In Hitler's case, it is all spelled out in his *Mein Kampf* (chapter 2). As a youth, he knew only one Jewish boy but had no particular feelings about him. As a teen, he encountered more arguments against Jews, but again, didn't make much out of them. It was not until he moved to Vienna in 1907 at the age of 18. Living there for six years, he personally encountered many Jews and learned much about their modes of operation: their control (and manipulation) of the press, their Marxism, their arrogance, their lies, their self-serving politics, their unkempt and malodorous appearance, their penchant for debasing culture, their role in crime and human trafficking… There was no end to the problems with Jews. "I gradually came to hate them," wrote Hitler. "From being a soft-hearted cosmopolitan, I became an out-and-out anti-Semite."

The threat posed by Jews was not merely to Germany or Europe, but indeed to all of humanity: "If the Jew, with the aid of his Marxist creed, were to triumph over the people of this world, his crown will be the funeral wreath of mankind." Thus for Hitler, the battle against Jewry took on something of a divine task—a mission to save the human race from virtual destruction. (Such a view was not unprecedented; some 150 years earlier, Voltaire said "[The Jews] are, all of them, born with a raging fanaticism in their hearts… I would not be in the least bit surprised if these people would not some day become deadly to the human race.")

20. What about World War One? What was the Jewish role in that catastrophic event?

This was another major source of Hitler's hatred: that Jews had a role in instigating the war, in the American involvement, and most importantly, in undermining Germany from within at a crucial moment, thus leading directly to German defeat. And, in the immediate aftermath, Jews rushed in to take hold of the levers of power in Germany.

Above we saw evidence that Jews dominated Germany and much of Europe throughout the 1800s. When Jews in Poland and Russia ran into governmental opposition, many fled to Germany, whose Jewish population rose from 510,000 in 1870 to 615,000 by 1910. Worse, many of these Jews took active roles in insurrection and revolution throughout Europe. Leading Zionist Jew Theodor Herzl wrote in 1897 that "when we sink [i.e. suffer persecution], we become a revolutionary proletariat, the subordinate officers of the revolutionary party." And indeed, Turkish Jews were very active in the Turkish Revolution of 1908 that overthrew the Sultan. The quarter-Jew Vladimir Lenin and full Jew Leon Trotsky played central roles in the failed Russian revolution of 1905, but Jewish assassins managed to kill Russian Interior Minister V. von Plehve in 1904 and Russian Prime Minister Pyotr Stolypin in 1911.

Vladimir Lenin   Leon Trotsky

In America, Woodrow Wilson was elected president in 1912 with massive Jewish support. As Henry Ford saw it, "Mr. Wilson, while president, was very close to the Jews. His administration, as everyone knows, was predominantly Jewish." Influential American Jews included Jacob Schiff, Louis Marshall, Paul Warburg, Bernard Baruch, Henry Morgenthau Sr, and Samuel Untermyer. They were instrumental in getting Wilson to enter the war in early 1917.

Jacob Schiff   Louis Marshall

Paul Warburg   Bernard Baruch

21. What was the significance of the Balfour Declaration?

Britain was losing badly to Germany for much of WWI, and they desperately needed help, especially from the nominally "neutral" Americans. British Jews knew they could activate their American brethren for help, but they wanted something in exchange: Palestine. And a victorious Britain would control Palestine. Therefore, England began negotiating with their Jewish Lobby in late 1916; if the American Jews could get the US into the war, the Brits would promise them their "homeland" in Palestine.

Immediately, powerful American Jews—as noted above—pressed Woodrow Wilson to declare war against Germany; and he did precisely this, in April 1917, despite the fact that the vast majority of Americans wanted to stay out of it. Keeping their side of the bargain, England then began negotiating a concise statement of intent, promising Palestine to the Zionist Jews. This promise ultimately took the form of a short letter—

one paragraph, actually—signed by England's Lord Balfour, in November 1917.

The Declaration is important because it proves that British Jews had the power to make a "contract" with the British government, and that American Jews had the power to bring the US into the war against the wishes of the American people. The same powerful Jewry that could do such things in WWI could certainly drive the same countries into war against Hitler.

Arthur Balfour

22. But what about Russia? Surely the Czar kept the Russian Jews in line.

Not really. As just mentioned, Lenin and Trotsky were very active in the failed revolt against Czar Nicholas II in 1905, but that event set the stage for the later, and entirely successful, revolution of 1917. In the aftermath of 1905, the potent Bolshevik movement (the more militant wing of the Marxists) became increasingly dominated by Jews; in addition to Lenin and Trotsky, there was Grigory Zinoviev, Yakov Sverdlov, Lev Kamenev, Karl Radek, Leonid Krassin, and Lazar Kaganovich. The *Times of London* reported as follows: "Of the 20 or 30 leaders who provide the central machinery of the Bolshevist movement, not less than 75% are Jews... Jews provide the executive officers."

It was these Bolshevik Jews that eventually succeeded, in March 1917, in driving the czar out of power; and later that year, they managed to seize control of the Russian government, thus completing their communist takeover of that nation. Jewish assassins then captured and executed the czar, his wife, and his five children in July 1918.

Czar Nicholas II

Even foreigners in Russia were not safe. In July of 1918, the German am-bassador to Russia, Wilhelm von Mirbach, was assassinated by a Jewish hitman, Yakov Blumkin. Yet another reason for Germans to hate Jews.

23. So, what role did Jews play in the defeat of Germany in WWI?
By 1918, the war had largely become a stalemate, with both sides en-trenched and little progress either way. But with the communist/Jewish takeover of Russia, they elected to sign a treaty with Germany and pull out of the war in March. This freed up many German troops, who could then be redeployed to the western front. It was a promising development.

But before the redeployment could have any effect, Jews and other communists within Germany began agitating for "peace," i.e. surrender, and thus an end to the war. A minor naval mutiny in late October grew into a general strike, promoted nationwide by Jews in two of the main German parties, the Social Democrats (SPD) and the Independent Social Democrats (USPD). Pressure grew rapidly on the German Kaiser Wil-helm II, and he finally abdicated in November.

The SPD then stepped in, formed a new "republic" government, and promptly surrendered. The war was over, and Germany had lost. Germa-ny had been "stabbed in the back" by the SPD Jews, and Hitler would never forgive them.

The USPD Jews, incidentally, had other ideas; they quickly moved to establish their own small "soviets," or regional governments. In north-ern Germany, the dominant Jews included Rosa Luxemburg, Hugo Haase, Karl Liebknecht, Karl Radek, and Alexander Parvus. In the south, the process was dictated by the likes of Kurt Eisner, Ernst Toller, and Gustav Landauer. But in the end, they were all killed, imprisoned, or driven out.

Rosa Luxemburg   Kurt Eisner

24. Why is all this important to the Holocaust?

Everything about World War Two, including the Holocaust, is grounded in events in World War One. We can never truly understand the Holocaust without understanding the many prior events that set the stage and prepared the groundwork.

Hitler fought as an infantryman for nearly the entire war and was recovering from a gas attack when the surrender occurred in late 1918. He was devastated. Upon hearing the news in a military hospital, he said, "I broke down completely." "I hadn't cried since the day I stood beside my mother's grave." But now he wept. The deaths of some two million German boys and men, all in vain. And all thanks to the Jews, "the originators of this crime."

This is what drove Hitler to enter politics; he vowed to right the wrongs of the "Great War." And the guilty parties were largely Jewish.

25. What did Hitler say in his "first letter" on the Jews?

At the age of 30, and not long after recovering from injuries he received in WWI, Hitler was asked to give his view on Jews in a brief letter of September 1919. In it, he emphasized that the Jews were first and foremost a race, not a religion, and thus that the matter is a racial question only. The Jew has shown himself to be "unscrupulous" and "merciless" in his quest for money; and thus "the result of his works is racial tuberculosis of the nation." The presence of Jews in a nation is like having a deadly illness.

We, therefore, must all become "rational anti-Semites": people who oppose Jews, not out of emotion or for religious reasons, but simply because they are a deadly danger to society. And the "final objective" of any such policy "must be the total removal of all Jews from our midst." Notice: not their imprisonment or death, but simply their *removal* from the nation. From his earliest years to the very end, this seems to have been the actual stance that Hitler held.

26. Didn't Hitler call for killing Jews in his book *Mein Kampf*?
Written in the mid-1920s, and covering two volumes and some 700 pages in English translation, *Mein Kampf* addresses a vast range of topics, from Hitler's early life and education to his views on politics, history, religion, and of course, the Jews. But in the entire work, he scrupulously avoids explicit calls to kill or even imprison masses of Jews.

There was only one small exception: late in Volume Two, Hitler recalls the role that Jews played, both in initiating World War One and in causing Germany's defeat in late 1918. If, he says, at the start of the war, "12,000 or 15,000 of these Hebraic corrupters" had been "held under poison gas"—as happened with so many Germans on the battlefield—that perhaps war could have been averted. Or at least, it could have ended in victory, thus saving potentially millions of lives. Such Jewish deaths, representing just one or two percent of the Jewish population at the time, could have checked the "tuberculosis" before it was too late. But this is the only such instance in the book; Hitler never calls for mass punishment of all Jews.

27. If Jews were active or even decisive in Germany's defeat in WWI, then it's likely that they played a large role in the post-war German government—is this true?
Yes, it is. Barely had the November 1918 surrender been signed than the dominant Jewish-led parties met in the city of Weimar, in early 1919, to create a new, "constitutional" form of government, one in which they would play a prominent role. Communist party leader Paul Levi joined hands with SPD leaders Otto Landesberg, Eduard Bernstein, and Rudolf

Hilferding, and they in turn invited Walter Rathenau and Hugo Preuss to join the group; all these men were Jews. A leading American journalist wrote about this a few years later: "In post-war [German] politics, any number of Jews rose to leadership. Both in the Reich and in the Federal States, Jews...became Cabinet Ministers. ... In short, after the [November] Revolution, the Jews came in Germany to play the same considerable part that they had previously [done]..."

28. Ok, but what about the cultural sphere: What role did Jews play there?

Weimar Germany was infamous for its cultural and moral depravity. A 1930s German scholar, Friedrich Wiehe, made this observation: "The World War, which had dire consequences for Germany, the following period of break-down of every political and economic order, the complete decay of the cultural life, the hollowing out of all virtues and moral values in all areas of life—this period of the deepest German degradation—coincided exactly with the completion of Jewish emancipation, with the height of Jewish power in Germany..."

British historian Arthur Bryant also wrote about the so-called Weimar "culture":

> Few of the Jews who set the spiritual and cultural fashions for Germany in the 1920s and early 1930s had any comprehension of a [German] point of view. ... They were exponents of the get-rich-quick philosophy [and] lovers of the flamboyant... [These Jews were] arrogant, they were vulgar, and they were vicious. ... It was not a pleasant thing in that period...to watch the throng of [German] children of both sexes who haunted the doors of the great Berlin hotels and restaurants to sell their bodies to rich [Jewish] *arrivistes*.

Berlin, recalled Bryant, had "lined the streets with the slogans of the brothel: 'A Thousand Naked Women!', 'Undress Yourselves!', 'Houses of Lust!'." He concludes: "The moral degradation of the German capital in those [Weimar] years had to be seen to be believed."

It was in reaction to this moral and cultural environment that Hitler and his National Socialist party grew in influence and power. Everywhere they looked, there were yet more reasons to hate Jews.

29. So it looks like Germany was dealing with Jews on many fronts: at home, in the Soviet Union, and even to the West—maybe in the US and Britain too; can this be right?
Absolutely. In a sense, Germany was faced with a Jewish problem on three fronts: in their domestic politics and the Weimar government; to the East, with the Soviet Bolsheviks initially led by Lenin and Trotsky; and in the Anglo world. Above we saw how powerful Jews dictated policy to Wilson and the US government, but there were equally influential Jews in England. There, men like Chaim Weizmann and Herbert Samuel held sway over a succession of prime ministers, including Ramsay MacDonald, Stanley Baldwin, and Neville Chamberlain—and later, Winston Churchill.

In the simplest terms, Germany had to deal with Weimar Jews (at home), communist Jews (in the USSR), and capitalist Jews (in the UK and USA).

Hitler's plan was this: drive out the German Jews, confront the Bolshevik Jews with a strong army, and make a peace treaty with the capitalist Jews in the West. But things didn't quite work out as planned.

Franklin D. Roosevelt

30. Was Roosevelt heavily influenced by Jews?
Franklin D. Roosevelt came to power in the US in early 1933, almost exactly at the same time that Hitler came to power in Germany (FDR

was seven years older). Hitler didn't know it at the time, but his counterpart FDR was steeped in Jewish influence from his earliest days. Back when he ran for governor of New York, his running mate was a Jew, Herbert Lehmann. Once in the governor's office, "he filled a number of key positions from the state's large Jewish population" (Shogan), including his longtime friend, Henry Morgenthau, Jr. Other early Jewish supporters included prominent lawyers Louis Brandeis and Felix Frankfurter.

Once in a position to run for president, FDR drew lots of Jewish support and Jewish money. "A number of wealthy Jewish friends contributed to Roosevelt's pre-nomination campaign fund" (Schonick), including Morgenthau, Lehmann, Jesse Straus, Laurence Steinhardt, and Bernard Baruch—the same Baruch who was given immense wartime powers under Woodrow Wilson during WWI. After he won the 1932 election, FDR proceeded to pack the White House with Jews: "his administration contained a higher proportion of Jews than any other," said Robert Michael. Bob Herzstein adds, "Jews were indeed more prominent than ever before in American history."

And to top it all off, FDR was himself likely part-Jewish, at least. He took great pains to hide this fact, but numerous clues leaked out over the years. In 1935, a former governor, Chase Osborn, wrote that "President Roosevelt knows well enough that his ancestors were Jewish. I heard Theodore Roosevelt state twice that his ancestors were Jewish." That would provide at least a partial explanation for his vast supplication to Jewish interests.

31. Churchill is always seen as a great hero of the British people; but is it really possible that he was funded and promoted by wealthy Jews?
Unquestionably, yes. Most British people from 1900 onward had no real antipathy toward Germany, other than as a potential competitor for economic power. We must recall that the British Empire was probably the dominant power on Earth, prior to World War One. The Brits didn't fear or hate anyone. But Churchill had several Jewish backers who did hate other nations—mostly, Czarist Russia and Germany under Kaiser Wilhelm II.

The entire Churchill family legacy seems to have benefitted from Jewish wealth. Some seven generations earlier, John Churchill (1650-1722) was funded in large part by a wealthy Jew, Solomon de Medina; it was Medina's money that helped establish the "aristocracy" of the Churchill family line. Winston's father, Randolph, was "excessively intimate" with Jewish banker Nathiel Rothschild and often conducted governmental business jointly with him. When Randolph died young at age 45 (from syphilis, contracted during an extramarital affair), his Jewish sponsors turned their attention to the 20-year-old Winston. Martin Gilbert, for example, explains that "after Randolph's death in 1895...[his] Jewish friends continued their friendship with the son. Lord [Nate] Rothschild, Sir Ernest Cassel, and Baron de Hirsch frequently invited him to their houses." Such "friends" were surely pleased when, in 1904, Winston opposed the immigration-limiting Aliens Bill when he was an MP for Manchester (Jews have always been pro-immigration, because it allows them free movement and also because it creates multiracial societies in which Jews thrive).

Winston Churchill

Churchill then made further important Jewish "friends," including the younger Lionel de Rothschild and Phillip Sassoon. And Cassel in particular provided considerable financial support, including furnishing two of Churchill's residences and generally managing his financial affairs. "Cassel's help to Churchill was continuous," said Gilbert; the elderly Jew offered him (in Churchill's own words) "unlimited credit."

Another prominent Jewish backer was Nathan Laski. As one of Churchill's "principal supporters" (Gilbert), Laski worked closely with Churchill to open Britain's borders to immigrants, especially Jewish ones. And Churchill also became good friends with the likes of strident Zionist Chaim Weizmann, and Moses Gaster. As he climbed the party ladder, he grew close to other influential Jews, including Jurgen Kuczynski and Leopold Schwarzschild. Unsurprisingly, Churchill repeatedly and consistently defended Jewish interests in parliament.

32. If so, then the Jews behind Churchill could have easily used him to push for war with Hitler, true?

Yes. By the mid-1930s, and after Hitler came to power in Germany, it was clear that British Jews were rabidly anti-German and wanted nothing more than to force the European nations into war to create a "regime change" in Germany and drive Hitler out. Consequently, Churchill too became rabidly anti-German and pro-war. And all the while, wealthy Jews curried favor with him, paying off his debts—Henry Strakosch gave him some 18,000 pounds in 1938—and supporting his lavish personal lifestyle. And Churchill was an important member of the secretive and obscure organization known as "the Focus," which was funded by Eugen Spier and other wealthy Jews, primarily to turn the neutral Brits against Hitler's Germany.

It is thus clear that Churchill was continuously goaded by wealthy Jews into becoming belligerent toward Hitler and Germany, and ultimately into fighting a war that his nation was ill-prepared to fight. Had there been no Churchill or wealthy Jews, England would likely have made a peace treaty with Hitler and saved themselves some 450,000 British lives and billions in expenses. And with no war on his western front, Hitler likely would have conquered the Soviet Union, sparing the world from Jewish-Bolshevik-communist terror and a future Cold War.

33. How did all this affect Hitler's rise to power?

It was increasingly clear to the German people that Jews were at the core of the Weimar decadence, and that Bolshevik Jews in the Soviet Union posed a potentially mortal threat, given that they had been slaughtering their internal enemies by the thousands since they came to power in 1917. The British Jews, working behind Churchill, were hell-bent on drumming up a war, as were FDR's Jews. Of all German parties, only Hitler's National Socialists were willing to speak the truth, call out the real enemy, and commit to tackling the problem head-on. The National

Socialists steadily increased their political standing throughout the 1920s and early 1930s, to the point where Hitler was named Chancellor on 30 January 1933.

Adolf Hitler

Once in power, he immediately began to recover Germany's economy; he tamed inflation, reduced unemployment, increased the GDP, built up the military, and restored a sense of pride to the German people. And he began the process of removing Jews from positions of power and influence. (Goebbels called it *entjudung*, or 'de-Jewing,' German society.) Jews, of course, were not happy; they called it "economic extermination"—something that would later morph into just plain "extermination." But they didn't flee, at least, not immediately; in 1933 there were some 520,000 Jews in Germany, about the same as in the 1870s and only slightly down from a peak of 600,000 in the 1910s.

34. Some say that the Jews actually declared a kind of 'war' on Hitler; is that true?
In a way, yes. On 24 March 1933, the British paper *Daily Express* carried a large headline: "Judea Declares War on Germany." It went on: "14 million Jews dispersed throughout the world have banded together as one man to declare war..." Jewish groups in the UK and America called for a global boycott of German goods; it was to be an "economic war," at least

at the start. Indeed, this boycott "was an international activity and can be understood as a type of Jewish foreign policy" (Vydra).

Later, into the late 1930s, we find more belligerence on the part of Jews, both in the UK and the US. Ben Ginsberg writes, "In the years before WW2, the efforts of the Jewish community helped in a number of important ways to bring isolationism [i.e pacifism] into disrepute and to turn American opinion against Germany. This, in turn, …helped to prepare the US for war." And in the UK, British ambassador to Germany Neville Henderson "sensed the situation he had long foreseen in which Jews, journalists, and the London intelligentsia would envelop diplomacy in a 'conflict of philosophies'" (Cowling), thus blocking all efforts at peace and reconciliation.

In December 1938, British Lord Beaverbrook wrote as follows:

> The Jews are after [Prime Minister] Chamberlain. He is being terribly harassed by them… All the Jews are against him… They have got a big position in the press here [in the UK]… I am shaken. The Jews may drive us into war [and] their political influence is moving us in that direction.

Then in August 1939, on the very brink of war, top British Jew Chaim Weizmann sent a letter to British Prime Minister Neville Chamberlain, in which he said:

> I wish to confirm in the most explicit manner the declarations which I and my colleagues have made during the last month, and especially last week: that the Jews stand by Great Britain and will fight on the side of the democracies. … The Jewish Agency is ready to enter into immediate arrangements for utilizing Jewish manpower, technical ability, and resources, etc. (*Times of London*, 6 Sep 1939, p. 8)

Chaim Weizmann

As Paul Rassinier observes, "this letter constituted a real declaration of war on Germany by the Jewish world, and created the problem of the internment of all German Jews in concentration camps." In other words, Hitler was completely justified at this point, just as he was entering Poland, to simultaneously begin rounding up Jews under his control and placing them in camps—just as America did with Japanese-Americans after Pearl Harbor.

35. What was the "Evian Conference"?
As soon as Hitler came to power in 1933, German Jews started to leave Germany, heading to other nations (there was no "Israel" yet). By 1938,

around 150,000 had left; but then Germany annexed Austria, and gained control of another 190,000 Jews. As the war-talk increased, more and more Jews sought to leave Germany. But where to go?

Thus, in July 1938, the French government convened a conference in the city of Evian to discuss the looming Jewish refugee situation, and specifically, to figure out where to send them. Delegates from 32 countries attended: Argentina, Australia, Belgium, Bolivia, Brazil, Canada, Chile, Colombia, Costa Rica, Cuba, Denmark, Dominican Republic, Ecuador, France, Guatemala, Haiti, Honduras, Ireland, Mexico, Netherlands, New Zealand, Nicaragua, Norway, Panama, Paraguay, Peru, Sweden, Switzerland, United Kingdom, United States, Uruguay, and Venezuela.

After a week of negotiations, the end result was that *only one country*—Dominican Republic—was willing to accept a small number of Jews; all the other nations, including the US, the UK, France, and Canada, refused to accept any. Apparently, the nations involved were not anxious to let in thousands of Jews, many of whom would have been Bolshevists, communists, or revolutionaries. This fact confirms what Hitler, Goebbels, and other leading Germans suspected: that the world, too, viewed the Jews as criminals and troublemakers, and were unwilling to let them in. In this way, the world essentially justified Germany's harsh treatment toward them.

36. Wasn't *Kristallnacht* in 1938 the actual start of the Holocaust?

No. *Kristallnacht* ('Crystal Night'), also called Night of the Broken Glass, was a one-night, nationwide series of riots against Jews—partly spontaneous and partly with the backing of a subgroup of the SA, but without endorsement from the top.

Again, the context is important. As noted above, there had been a standing Jewish 'war' against Germany for over five years, and the global boycott had significant negative effects on ordinary Germans. That, and the constant Jewish agitating against Hitler were an ongoing irritant. Then on 7 November 1938, a 29-year-old German diplomat in France named Ernst vom Rath was shot and killed by a Jewish teenager, Herschel Grynszpan. (More reason to hate Jews.) This seems to have been the last straw. As a consequence, several anti-Jewish riots broke out two days later; in the end, over 250 synagogues and 7,000 Jewish businesses were damaged or destroyed, and some 90 Jews were killed. The German public was demanding action against the German Jews. Hitler then complied, issuing mass-arrest warrants and collectively fining the Jews 1 billion marks.

Ernst vom Rath   Herschel Grynszpan

There is no evidence at all that Hitler ordered the riots, nor that he even wanted them. The death toll (90) was tragic but minuscule compared to later alleged Holocaust actions. And virtually no conventional historians argue for this as the start of that event. By all accounts, the top Germans were not terribly upset about the actions but, at the same time, were happy to be done with it; as Goebbels wrote in his diary, "Good that it's over."

37. World War Two technically began in September 1939. But is it really possible that British Jews, for example, pushed England into war with Germany?
It's more than possible; it actually happened—and we have several testimonies to this effect. Churchill was very antagonistic toward Hitler, thanks largely to the belligerence of the wealthy Jews who were backing him. In 1936, long before any threat of war, Churchill remarked, "Germany is getting too strong. We must smash her." But why? In 1938, Polish ambassador Jerzy Potocki reported that "The Jews are right now the leaders in creating a war psychosis which would plunge the entire world into war and bring about general catastrophe." That same year, influential American Jew Barney Baruch told General Marshall, "We are going to lick that fellow Hitler. He isn't going to get away with it." And Churchill himself told Baruch, "War is coming very soon. We will be in

it and you [Americans] will be in it." How could he have known this in 1938, when war would not start until late in 1939?

Beyond this, we must note that Germany began the war by crossing into Polish territory in an attempt to recover land lost in prior battles. The 'original' war was simply Germany against Poland (with the USSR joining in, also against Poland, two weeks later). And yet, two days into the war, it was *England* that declared war on *Germany*. At the prodding of British and American Jews, Chamberlain had unwisely given Poland a "security guarantee" in March of 1939 that promised "all support in their power" in case Germany attacked. His statement was short and vague, and didn't really carry force of law, but it was enough to compel England to declare war six months later—which was the fervent wish of Churchill and his Jewish backers, despite the will of the British people and despite the fact that England was in no position at that time to take on the Germans.

38. But was this really the doing of Jews or simply belligerent Brits?
All evidence points to the Jews as the driving force. It seems strange in retrospect, but the Americans, Brits, Poles, and most Jews thought that Germany would be "an easy mark"; all they had to do was work together and somehow initiate a war, and Germany would be crushed—thus simultaneously ending the "Hitler threat" and reasserting Jewish dominance in the world. It turned out to be not so easy.

By early 1939, well before the war, it was something of an open secret that Western Jews were pushing hard for war. Retired US general George Moseley said "The war now proposed is for the purpose of establishing Jewish hegemony throughout the world." By mid-year, US ambassador Joseph Kennedy (father of JFK) exclaimed that "Jews were running the United States" and that "the democratic policy of the US is a Jewish production." A month later, the British ambassador to Germany told Hitler, "the hostile attitude in Great Britain was the work of Jews and enemies of the Nazis."

At least Hitler understood something of the cause of Western belligerence when he authorized the Polish invasion on 1 September 1939. The Jews hated him and wanted him gone, and they would do whatever they had to, including driving neutral, peaceful nations into war, often against their will, and often using trickery and deceit.

PART 4

THE START OF "THE HOLOCAUST"

39. When did the Holocaust actually begin?

This is entirely unclear, and even our professional historians cannot agree. Some claim that "the Holocaust" includes all Jewish oppression under Hitler, which, they say, began as soon as he came to power in January 1933—even though there would be no "systematic killing" for years. Some say it started with the Nuremburg Laws of 1935 that formalized the opposition to German Jewry, but without taking direct action against them. Some point to *Kristallnacht* of 10 November 1938 (see above), but this event caused little direct harm to the mass of German Jews.

Some say it began, at least in principle, upon Hitler's famous speech of 30 January 1939, when he issued his "prophecy" that if the Jews of the world drove him into war, that the result would be the *Vernichtung* (destruction, elimination) of the European Jews. But this was a major public speech and Hitler would never have announced any planned, and top-secret, "Holocaust" in such a public forum. An honest reading of his words shows that he intended to crush Jewish power in Europe (which was considerable) and to drive them out, voluntarily or involuntarily. We must remind ourselves that Hitler never, in speeches or in writing, in public or in private, ever discussed actually killing the Jews. It was never his plan and never his intent. But he did repeatedly speak of crushing their collective power and dominance in society.

Other historians point to the start of the war in September 1939; or to the date of the German attack on the Soviet Union in June 1941; or to opening of the Chełmno transit camp in December 1941; or to the infamous Wannsee Conference in January 1942. A plausible case can be made for the June 1941 date, as we will see below.

40. So Hitler only intended to remove the Jews from Germany, not kill them?

Yes, that's correct. This is the "Deportation Thesis" described earlier. As early as 1931, the Germans discussed plans to transfer out the roughly 500,000 Jews that lived in Germany. One popular alternative was the island of Madagascar, off the coast of Africa. In January 1938, the vehemently anti-Jewish journal *Der Stürmer* wrote that they "suggested some years ago that a way to solve the Jewish Question would be to transport the Jews to the French colony of Madagascar." "Today," they continued, "our proposal is being discussed by foreign statesmen." In his personal diary of 11 April 1938, Goebbels wrote, "The Fuhrer wants to push the Jews completely out of Germany. To Madagascar, or some such place. Right!" And he added a few days later: "The Fuhrer wants to deport them [Jews] all step by step. … Madagascar would be the most suitable for them."

Joseph Goebbels

Eventually the "Madagascar Plan" was formalized, and in July 1940 it was presented to the German leadership. It said:

> The approaching victory gives Germany the possibility …
> of solving the Jewish Question in Europe. The desirable so-
> lution is: all Jews out of Europe. … France must make the
> island of Madagascar available for the solution of the Jew-
> ish Question… The island will be transferred to Germany
> under a mandate. … Apart from this, the Jews will have
> their own administration in this territory: their own mayors,
> police, postal, and railroad administration, etc. … Moreo-
> ver, the Jews will remain in German hands as a pledge for

the future good behavior of the members of their race in America.

Clearly there was no plan to kill them—in fact, here was a reason *not* to kill them: as insurance against American hostility.

For various reasons, the plan was never enacted, unfortunately. But it was actively discussed well into 1942. As late as March of that year, Goebbels wrote in his diary: "There are still 11 million Jews in Europe. They will have to be concentrated later, to begin with, in the East; possibly an island, such as Madagascar, can be assigned to them after the war." Again, no plan to kill Jews—even in March 1942!

41. But surely many Jews died during Hitler's reign, did they not?
Of course. Sometimes we have to remind ourselves of the obvious: people die all the time. They die from old age, disease, injury, and accident. They die from homicide, and they die from suicide. In any sufficiently large population group, about 1% die of such causes every year. Therefore, of the roughly 500,000 German Jews living under Hitler in the pre-war years, about 5,000 would have died every year, no matter what Hitler did. Many Jews left Germany throughout the 1930s, and the population dropped to about 200,000 by 1939—thus, by that time, annual deaths were down to about 2,000.

So, between 1933 and the start of the war in 1939, we can estimate that 25,000 Jews died in total. And we can be sure that every one was counted as a "Holocaust death."

42. But that's not what people mean by a "Holocaust death," is it?
We don't really know, because our experts never really tell us who died of what cause, and when. They simply refuse to explain what counts as a "Holocaust victim."

43. That's hard to believe; the Holocaust has been called "the most well-documented event in history"; surely the experts know, in great detail, when, where, and how the 6 million Jews died—don't they?
If they know, they aren't saying. Virtually no official documented source shows us when, where, and how the Jews died under Hitler, coming to a

total of 6 million. It is a very basic matter, and yet no expert seems able to provide this information. This fact is hugely revealing.

44. How do the revisionists address this problem?
They must piece together the story using the best available information from a variety of expert sources. It ends up being something of a puzzle —how to account for the alleged 6 million Jewish deaths. For a good discussion of this situation, see Dalton's book *Debating the Holocaust*.

45. So, how many Jews allegedly died *before* the war, on the standard view?
Based on best estimates of the Extermination Thesis, around 100,000 Jews died in Germany between 1933 and 1939, and another 20,000 in 1940. Something like this is required to reach the 6-million total. Of these, perhaps 35,000 or 40,000 are said to have been killed outright, for various reasons (as criminals, traitors, thieves, etc.), over eight years. But again, this is for our experts to confirm; and they refuse to do so.

46. What is the corresponding revisionist estimate?
In the pre-war period, according to revisionism, virtually all Jewish deaths were of natural causes. Hence the revisionist total is the figure cited above: about 25,000.

47. So the standard version is about five times as high as the revisionist claim—true? Some might say, exaggerated by a factor of five?
Yes. Again, this is just for the pre-war deaths. Revisionists argue that the standard figures for all the various aspects of the Holocaust are typically between five and ten times too high.

48. But even if we accept the figure of 100,000 pre-war, this means that the vast majority of the Holocaust victims—of the 6 million— died between 1941 and 1945, isn't that right?
True. On the Extermination Thesis, 98% of all Jewish deaths occurred between January 1941 and the end of the war in May 1945. Thus, the pre-war deaths are nearly irrelevant.

49. Okay, so, for each year of the war, how many Jews died?
Again, revisionists need to construct these numbers because the orthodox experts refuse to give them to us. If we are to reach a total of 6 million, then something close to the following figures must be true:

- 1941 = 950,000 Jewish deaths
- 1942 = 3.4 million deaths
- 1943 = 750,000 deaths
- 1944 = 700,000 deaths
- 1945 = 80,000 deaths

50. And what are the corresponding figures from the revisionists?
Those would be:

- 1941 = 90,000 Jewish deaths
- 1942 = 260,000 deaths
- 1943 = 100,000 deaths
- 1944 = 75,000 deaths
- 1945 = 20,000 deaths

Again, these are very rough estimates, based on the best available data and existing forensic evidence.

51. That is still a lot of deaths, isn't it? That's still a tragedy.
Of course. But any major war is a tragedy. Something like 60 million people died overall in World War Two. This was a war that did not have to happen, and wouldn't have happened, without constant pressure from warmongering Jews in the UK and the USA.

It is an extreme irony: Most of the Jewish deaths occurred precisely *because* there was a major war. Before the war, there were no concentration camps, no mass shootings, no typhus epidemics—none of the things that accounted for most Jewish deaths. If Hitler had not had to fight England and France, and eventually the US, and instead earned a quick victory against Stalin, most of those Jewish deaths could have been avoided. In a very real sense, *the Jews caused their own Holocaust*.

PART 5

THE GAS CHAMBERS

52. Is it true that Hitler gassed 6 million Jews?

Of course not—not even according to the exterminationist thesis. Since we constantly hear about those "homicidal gas chambers," we need to look hard at the ways in which Jews died.

On the orthodox view, the 6 million deaths can be divided into three main categories: *ghetto deaths*, *mass shootings* (mostly in the captured Soviet territory), and *concentration camps* (including the so-called "death camps"). The estimated deaths are as follows:

1) Ghetto deaths = 1 million
2) Shootings = 1.6 million
3) Camps = 3.4 million

As we can see, these add up to 6 million. Revisionists, of course, dispute all three figures and claim that they are exaggerated by a factor of eight or ten.

We have very little factual information on the first category. There were hundreds of ghettos in larger Germany, up to 1,000 or more, large and small. Thousands of Jews were confined in them, mostly between 1941 and 1943, and thousands surely died—again, most of disease or natural causes. But we have no material evidence even approaching the alleged 1 million deaths.

53. Who conducted all those shooting deaths?

Most were by the German military units called the *Einsatzgruppen* ("mission groups"). As soon as Germany attacked the Soviet Union in June 1941, these groups were established to protect the front-line troops from being attacked from the rear—mostly by militant Jews, as it turns out. To keep the troops safe, thousands of partisan Jews were rounded up and shot. This was the first true mass-killing of Jews, and thus can plausibly be considered the start of the "Holocaust." Again, these were not, by and large, innocent civilians; they were complicit in lethal action against German soldiers.

However, our expert historians are conflicted regarding how many Jews were actually shot by the Einsatzgruppen. The Israeli Holocaust institute (Yad Vashem) says 1.25 million; expert Raul Hilberg claims 1.4 million; the US Holocaust Memorial Museum (USHMM) says up to 2 million; and Catholic priest Patrick Desbois has claimed 2.2 million.

54. That's a huge variation—why can't the experts agree?
Good question. Either they are confused, mistaken, or lying.

55. So where did the estimate of 1.6 million (above) come from?
That's a rough average of the orthodox figures. Revisionists, by contrast, believe that something like 140,000 or 150,000 Jews were shot on the eastern front.

56. Back to the gas chambers: If 2.6 million died in ghettos or shootings, then all the "camp" deaths (3.4 million) were gassed, right?
Wrong. Again, we need some detail. Of all the camp fatalities, most allegedly occurred in just six notorious "death camps": Chełmno, Belzec, Sobibor, Treblinka, Majdanek, and Auschwitz. Just these six camps account for 88% (3 million) of the 3.4 million "camp" total.

57. What about Birkenau? Isn't that considered a famous death camp?
Birkenau was a sub-camp of Auschwitz, and is considered to be part of that larger camp complex.

58. So those six death-camp totals were all gassing deaths?
No, but close. The first four listed above were all gassing deaths, according to our experts. Majdanek allegedly had some 75,000 Jewish victims but only 14,000 of these were gassed. And in Auschwitz, of the 1 million alleged Jewish deaths, 90% were said to be gassed and 10% died in other ways.

59. So, how many alleged gassing victims in all?
About 2.8 million in total—just under half of the 6 million.

60. But revisionists disagree; how many gassing victims do they claim?
Zero! This is perhaps the most shocking disagreement, and it gets to the heart of the Holocaust controversy.

First, we need to be clear what we mean by "gassing." There were two alleged methods, both very different: (1) using hydrogen cyanide gas, stored in the form of granular pellets (called "Zyklon-B"), and (2) using carbon monoxide gas, typically generated by diesel engines. Method 1 is claimed at Auschwitz; method 2 is claimed for the other five camps. Unfortunately for the Extermination Thesis, both methods would have been virtually unworkable and impossible, as described by witnesses; details below.

Also, we must note that many camps did indeed use poisonous Zyklon gas, but in every case, it was as a pesticide to kill disease-bearing lice. Typhus was a major problem during the war, and many camps used Zyklon to limit the spread of the disease and thus to *save* inmate lives, not end them. This is yet another case where the truth is the opposite of what has been claimed.

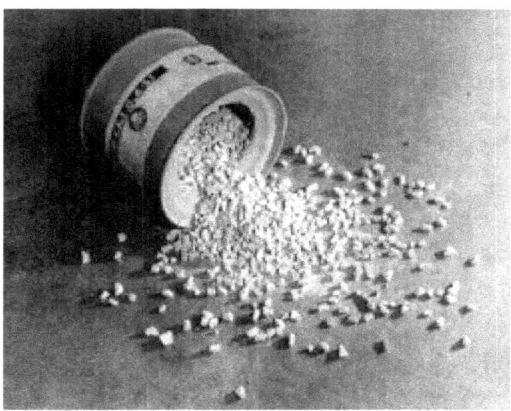

Zyklon-B

Here, the reality is that we have (a) no documentation about homicidal gas chambers; (b) no writings by Hitler, Goebbels, or anyone regarding such chambers; (c) no remaining physical evidence of such chambers; and (d) no autopsies showing death by gassing. All that we do have are so-called witnesses, mostly Jewish inmates, who saw or heard about: *dead bodies* (true, mostly from typhus), *functioning crematoria* (true, for burning those who died), *Zyklon gas* (true, for killing lice), and *fellow Jews "disappearing"* (true, as people died or were transferred out of camps). All stories of homicidal gas chambers are essentially rumors that were innocently, or maliciously, passed along, based on fragments of information.

In reality, there were *no* homicidal gas chambers at *any* camp under German control; this is the logical conclusion from everything that we know today.

61. Wait, so why couldn't diesel engine gas be used to kill people?

Regarding diesel engines, many camps did indeed have diesel generators to produce electricity. And many camps used diesel trucks for transportation, which were very common at that time. But the use of diesel exhaust to kill people is all but impossible, precisely because that exhaust gas contains very low amounts of the deadly carbon monoxide (unlike regular gasoline engines, which produce a lot). A diesel would have to be rigged to run at very high speeds, while stationary, and under a very heavy load, to even begin to produce high levels of CO gas. It would have made no sense to even try.

Furthermore, the people were allegedly crowded into "hermetically sealed" rooms and the engine gas was then pumped in. But this would never work, because you can't pump gas into a sealed room—the pressure would just increase until the walls collapsed or the engine stalled.

And in any case, if you had an air-tight room, you don't need a "gas" at all. Just pack the victims in, seal the doors, and wait about an hour—all would be dead from asphyxiation. This would have been far simpler, easier, and safer for the Germans.

62. Is it possible that the Germans actually used regular gasoline engines?

In theory, yes, and in fact a few people claim this is what happened at Sobibor. Gasoline engines do produce enough CO gas to kill people relatively quickly. But again, the Germans would have had the same situation mentioned above: you can't pump engine gas into a sealed room, and if you had such a room, you wouldn't even bother with the gas.

63. How did the Germans supposedly use the Zyklon-B pellets at Auschwitz?

According to former inmates, some of the gas chamber rooms had holes punched in the ceiling, and then SS men went up and sprinkled the deadly pellets on the heads of the Jews in the room below. In other alleged chambers, the SS men used high windows on a side wall to dump in the pellets.

But this whole story fails, for several reasons: (1) no SS man could just open a can of deadly Zyklon pellets without a full-body suit equipped with gas mask; but no one has ever found or described such a thing; (2) the pellets would fall in basically one spot, and thus could not readily release their gas; it would have taken far too long; (3) if you sprinkle loose pellets on people to kill them, after they die, you have dead bodies intermixed with gas-emitting pellets, which would continue to release their gas for an hour or two; there would be no way to collect the pellets, clear out the poison gas, and extract the dead bodies, without workers being themselves killed. The whole process would take an entire day or more—which does not meet the requirement of a high-speed "assembly line" approach to mass murder, like we are told.

64. Weren't the crematoria used to kill Jews?

No. A crematorium is any facility used to incinerate dead bodies and reduce them to ash. They are very common all around the world today. But a crematorium works only on corpses, not living people. It would have been insane to try to force live people into the tiny oven openings, each of which could hold one body at a time, and took around an hour to fully incinerate. No witnesses anywhere claim that live people were killed in a crematorium. What they do claim is that the "gas chambers" were located right next to the crematoria, to make it easy to dispose of the dead bodies. But this is nonsense because the "gas chambers" never could have functioned, as explained above.

65. But we have Germans themselves who admitted to gassing people, don't we?

Yes, some such records do exist, but they were all captive Germans, after the war, who were imprisoned and tortured into saying many ridiculous things, simply to please their captors or to hope for a lesser punishment.

Any "confessions" by tortured inmates are worthless. What we would need is some physical evidence: documents, plans, photos, actual chamber remains, etc. But we have nothing.

66. So, is it true that the only logical conclusion is that there were no homicidal gas chambers at all, in the German camps?
Yes, absolutely. No homicidal chambers, and hence zero gassing victims. The alleged figure of 2.8 million is absurd. No Jews died in gas chambers. Many died in other ways, but none in gas chambers.

67. So what happened to those 2.8 million Jews?
Some died of typhus, some were surely shot, and many were transferred out of the "death camps" and sent to work camps in the far east. When the Soviets recaptured huge amounts of territory in the later years of the war, they would have also captured many thousands of Jews—perhaps hundreds of thousands—who had been shipped to the East. Then after the war, when the Iron Curtain came down, those thousands of Jews were "lost" to the west and never heard from again.

And of course, many Jews were liberated from their camps by the Allies and survived long after the war—long enough to tell their stories of the "death camps" and "gas chambers." This partly explains why, even today, we have so many "Auschwitz survivors."

PART 6

A CLOSER LOOK AT THE DEATH CAMPS

68. We are told that there were six main death camps, that together accounted for around half of the 6 million alleged deaths. How many died at each camp?

Again, we get widely varying figures from our so-called experts, so it is hard to say for sure. However, if we take rough averages for each camp, we get something like the following numbers:

- Chełmno = 250,000
- Belzec = 550,000
- Sobibor = 225,000
- Treblinka = 900,000
- Majdanek = 75,000
- Auschwitz = 1 million

A quick check shows that these add up to exactly 3 million—half of the Holocaust.

69. But, as usual, the revisionists must disagree; what figures do they support?

Based on a variety of revisionist sources, we can estimate the following numbers:

- Chełmno = 2,000
- Belzec = 40,000
- Sobibor = 10,000
- Treblinka = 25,000
- Majdanek = 28,000
- Auschwitz = 140,000

These figures add up to 245,000—a vastly lower number than above. From the revisionist perspective, the orthodox experts have exaggerated the camp deaths by a factor of 12.

70. Let's look quickly at each of the first five camps, and then later focus on Auschwitz. Take Chełmno—what do we know about that camp?
Almost nothing, actually. There is very little remaining documentation. One noted revisionist, Jürgen Graf, writes, "Of Chełmno, we know next to nothing." Another prominent revisionist, Carlo Mattogno, agrees: "Documentation about it is almost nonexistent." This is largely because Chełmno wasn't even really an actual camp, like the others; it was more of a processing center and, separately, a burial ground. Allegedly, Jews were transported to Chełmno and then herded into special transit vans. These vans were allegedly modified to send the engine exhaust into the rear cabin area, where the Jews would be gassed. The van then drove the dead bodies a few miles away for burning and burial. This is the "gas van" myth.

Any such van as described would have had a diesel engine, and as we saw above, diesels put out far too little carbon monoxide to kill people in any reasonable time. And, also as we saw, one cannot pump engine exhaust into an enclosed compartment; either the compartment will explode or the engine will die. So revisionists are virtually certain that the gas van stories are false.

71. But lots of people are claimed to have been killed this way, true?
Yes, there have been outrageous claims—claims that vary widely. Orthodox historian Martin Gilbert tells us that 360,000 people (!) were killed at Chełmno; Yad Vashem says 320,000; Esther Goldberg's "Holocaust Memoir Digest" claims 250,000; the USHMM tells us that "over 152,000" died there; and researcher Jean-Claude Pressac argues for under 85,000.

72. That's a huge variation—why can't the experts agree?
Good question.

73. But revisionists say: only 2,000?
Or so. There is so little data, such a lack of remains, no viable means of killing, on and on. Two thousand is a very rough guess, almost like saying, none at all.

74. How long did it allegedly take the Germans to kill, say, 250,000 people in "gas vans"?

According to our experts, just nine months: January through September 1942. This means that they would have had to kill almost 28,000 people per month, or 925 per day, on average—every day, rain or shine, for nine straight months.

75. Not only that—how did they get rid of all those bodies?

Here we find more bizarre statements. At first, the Germans allegedly buried all those bodies in deep pits in the nearby forest (there is a "memorial site" there today). But then, just as the nine months of gassing was coming to a close, someone in the German hierarchy decided to dig up and burn the bodies—perhaps to "destroy the evidence." Why the Germans would care about evidence at that point, no one can say.

So, as we are told, the Germans spent the next five months burning corpses—around 50,000 per month, or about 1,600 per day.

Now, this would have presented an insurmountable problem: Here they are, in the middle of a forest in the Polish countryside, and the men have to dig up, and burn—out in the open—1,600 bodies per day, every day, rain or shine. They have to find wood for the fire; they have to stack the bodies on some kind of "grill"; they have to keep the fire burning hot; and then they have to get rid of all the wood and body ash—all in one day, just to do the same thing all over again the next day.

Just consider the wood needed. One average corpse requires about 350 pounds (160 kg) of wood to completely incinerate. (They were not "cooking" the bodies, *they were burning them completely to ash*.) So, 1,600 bodies would require about 560,000 pounds of wood *each day*. An average large pine or maple tree contains about 4,000 pounds of usable firewood; thus, the Germans would have needed to chop, trim, and cut up about 140 trees per day, every day, for five months. This is absurd.

76. If that actually happened, then there would be (1) large, former pits, now refilled with dirt, (2) a large deforested area, and (3) tons and tons of ash. Do we have any evidence of all that?

Nothing close to what we would expect. According to one expert, Patrick Montague, the ash was "simply buried in pits four meters deep and eight to ten meters wide." If so, it is still there; ash persists in the ground for centuries, even millennia. But four excavations over the years have found nothing like the required ash. The "pits" that are marked out today were never scanned to see how deep they are. And there are no acres of deforested land; in fact, the grave area is quite heavily forested today, and not with youngish trees.

Chełmno camp burial ground (today)

And it's actually worse than that. In open-air fires, the flames cannot get hot enough to totally consume an entire body. In particular, hard parts, like teeth and large bones, will survive even hours of burning. Therefore, amongst all that ash would be the teeth and large-bone fragments from 250,000 people. Just think of it: something like *8 million teeth* should still be in the ground today, waiting to be dug up and used as proof of "Nazi barbarity." Instead, we have no teeth at all—or at least, none that the authorities are willing to show us.

77. Let's look at the other camps. Belzec, Sobibor, and Treblinka are often grouped together; why is that?

These three camps are considered part of a German plan called "Operation Reinhardt," in which Jews would be transferred to transit camps in the east of German-controlled Poland, disinfested of lice, and then shipped further east, to labor camps or other concentration camps in the captured Soviet territory. All three camps were of similar design and operation. All were located on the border between the former Poland and the captured Soviet territory.

Treblinka camp memorial

From all the data and evidence that we have, these camps functioned largely as planned. Thousands of Jews were sent there by train from all over Europe. They were disinfested of lice, and then moved on further east. Once leaving these three camps, the Jews were officially "removed" from German territory and henceforth considered "ex-terminated"—that is, pushed out beyond the boundaries of the Reich.

The three camps began operation in spring to summer of 1942, and ran until April 1943 (Belzec), July 1943 (Treblinka), and September 1943 (Sobibor). By late 1943, the Soviets were recapturing much territory and Jewish transports to the East were no longer feasible.

78. How many Jews are claimed to have been killed at those camps?
As always, there is a wide range of answers. Sobibor is alleged to have killed between 150,000 (Hilberg) and 350,000 (Bauer/Zimmerman) Jews; Belzec, between 434,000 (USHMM) and 1 million (Tregenza);

and Treblinka, between 750,000 (Van Pelt) and 1.2 million (Noakes and Pridham).

79. Those are huge variations—why can't the experts agree?
Good question.

80. If these camps were located in remote wooded areas, they probably had all the same problems that Chełmno did, is that correct?
Yes. The gassing rates would have been very high: 12,000 per month at Sobibor; 55,000 per month at Belzec; and an astonishing *81,000 per month* at Treblinka. And all using diesel engine exhaust, allegedly. The problems would have been insurmountable. Such figures are sheer fantasy.

Then they would have had to burn all those bodies, in the open air, with no crematorium: 20,000 per month at Sobibor, 110,000 per month at Belzec, and an astounding *220,000 per month* at Treblinka. And with all the same problems: tons of firewood, tons of ash, teeth and bone remains, and so on. It simply could not have happened in the manner described.

Finally, we have, again, an utter lack of physical evidence: no remains of gas chambers, no deep burial pits, no ash, no teeth, no bones. Given this, even the much lower revisionist estimates are questionable; the actual figures could be lower still.

81. Majdanek camp seems relatively insignificant: just 75,000 deaths from the experts, and only 28,000 from revisionists. Was the camp always so unimportant?
No. At one time, over 1.5 million people (including Jews) were claimed to have been killed there (*New York Times*, and Deborah Lipstadt). This would have made it worse than Auschwitz. But gradually the "official estimates" started coming down: to 360,000 (Laqueur), to 235,000 (Rajca), to 170,000 (Kranz), to 80,000 Jews (Kranz again), to, now, just 59,000 Jews (Kranz yet again). This is a 96% reduction from the original figures, and now a mere 1% of the 6 million.

From the revisionist side, the 28,000 Jewish deaths make the camp worse than Chełmno, Sobibor, and even Treblinka—but significantly below Belzec and Auschwitz, which are now the "Big Two."

Majdanek camp today

Still, Majdanek is an instructive case; it shows how, under revisionist pressure, the death figures have come down dramatically. If the other camps had similar reductions, we would be much closer to reality.

82. Let's turn to the big fish in the pond: Auschwitz. Didn't the experts used to claim that 4 million people were killed there, instead of the 1 million or so today?

That is correct—actually, it was even worse than that. Near the end of the war, the *New York Times* splashed a big headline: "5,000,000 reported slain at Oswiecim" (12 April 1945, p. 6; Oswiecim is the Polish name for Auschwitz). It said that a Dr. Bela Fabian "accused the Germans today of having killed 5,000,000 Jews at the Oswiecim extermination camp in Polish Silesia." A few years later, the French paper *Le Monde* listed the death toll as 4.7 million. But it was a 1945 Soviet report, in which they stated that 4 million persons had died, which became the orthodox source. Again, no one bothered to actually investigate, to look for remains, and so on.

The 4-million figure held in official circles all the way to 1990. Then, on July 17, the figure changed overnight. As the *Washington Times* reported:

> Poland has cut its estimate of the number of people killed by the Nazis in the Auschwitz death camp from 4 million to just over 1 million. ... Shevach Weiss, a death camp survivor and Labor Party member of the Israeli Parliament,

expressed disbelief at the revised estimates, saying, "It sounds shocking and strange." … The latest Polish research is based on studies of prisoners' personal numbers, transport documents and data about Jewish ghettos. (p. A11)

5,000,000 REPORTED SLAIN AT OSWIECIM

Hungarian Liberated by U. S. Troops Says Jews Were Killed Over 10 Months

NEAR ERFURT, Germany, April 11 (UP)—Dr. Bela Fabian, president of the dissolved Hungarian Independent Democratic party, accused the Germans today of having killed 5,000,000 Jews at the Oswiecim extermination camp in Polish Silesia, from which he himself narrowly escaped.

[The Polish Ministry of Information reported more than a year ago that 500,000 Jews had been gassed and cremated at this camp and the International Church Movement's ecumenical refugee committee, in a subsequent report on Oswiecim and its sister camp of Birkenau, said that 1,715,000 Jews had been killed at the two places. A spokesman for the American Jewish Committee's library in New York said that it had been estimated that 4,000,000 to 5,000,000 Jews had been exterminated since the war began in Europe, but the library had no figures to substantiate a report that 5,000,000 had been exterminated in one camp.]

Dr. Fabian declared that the executions had been carried out during ten months. He said all Jews more than 50 years old had been automatically condemned to the gas chamber and crematory, as were the weak and young mothers who refused to leave their children. "If the captain did not like the looks of anyone else, he was gassed too," he said.

Many died of overwork, starvation and beatings before the gas chamber could receive them, Dr. Fabian said. The officer in charge, he continued, employed a dramatic flourish of the hand in ordering entire groups taken away to be gassed and cremated — without questioning or examining them to learn whether they were guilty of any wrong.

The 56-year-old author and politician told his story of the notorious camp, since captured by the Red Army, after his liberation by American troops from another camp at Ohrdruf, southwest of Erfurt. Three others liberated with Dr. Fabian corroborated his story and said that it was a "miracle" that he still lived. They said that he owed his life to the fact that the Germans believed him when he said that he was only 46 years old. The three others are Heinz Meyer, 22, a Hungarian violinist; Desider Kohlmann, 34, a Slovak, and Sam Ezratty, 28, a Greek medical student.

Dr. Fabian, who said that he had once had lunch with President Roosevelt, asked that Representative Sol Bloom, Democrat, of New York, be notified that he was safe. He is the author of two books, "One Thousand Men Without a Woman" and "Six Horses and Forty Men."

83. So, the "6 million" must have also been affected—dropping to … 3 million?

Actually, no. The 6 million never changes, no matter what. Here's what happened: The authorities declared that, of the old figure of 4 million, there were 1 million Jews and 3 million others (Poles, Slavs, etc.). But the "latest research" showed that the 3 million others were really more like 100,000. So the number of Jews did not change; it stayed at around 1 million. Therefore, no change to the 6 million—amazing!

Entrance to Auschwitz main camp

84. Let's say we accept the standard figure of 1 million. When and how were those people killed?

For our purposes here, Auschwitz may be considered to have two main parts: the main camp and the much larger Birkenau sub-camp, a few miles away. Both camps allegedly began gassing Jews in early 1942: in Crematorium #1 of the main camp, and in two converted farmhouses ("bunkers") in Birkenau. By the end of that first year of 1942, Crema #1 had gassed around 20,000 Jews, and the two bunkers around 140,000—thus, 160,000 total for the year.

Into 1943, Birkenau got four new crematoria (#2 - #5). So the bunkers were largely decommissioned, and all the gassing action shifted to Birkenau; for that year, another 160,000 or so gassing victims in all.

But 1944 was really the standout year. Nearly 600,000 Jews were allegedly gassed that year alone—an average of 50,000 per month or about 1,600 per day.

85. Wait—1,600 people gassed per day? Every day, for an entire year? That sounds impossible.

Indeed. Actually, it is worse than that: For just a single two-month period, mid-May to mid-July, the experts tell us that an astounding 300,000 people were gassed—mostly (allegedly) the Hungarian Jews who were recently deported to Auschwitz. This comes to an incredible 5,000 people per day, for two solid months. And that's just the average; at the worst point, some *10,000 people* were gassed per day. At least, that's what our so-called experts tell us.

86. And all with Zyklon gas?
Yes—and thus all the problems that come with that: poisonous cans that can't be safely opened, no feasible way to get the pellets in so that they actually work, no way to get the pellets out quickly and safely, no way to aerate the room, and so on.

Birkenau Gate House

87. But the crematorium buildings had actual gas chamber rooms in them, didn't they?
No. What they had were large storage rooms, some half-underground, in which the Germans would store the corpses prior to incineration.

We must remember that Auschwitz (plus Birkenau) was a very large facility, holding something like 135,000 inmates at its peak. And there was a typhus epidemic raging at the time, especially in 1944. Hundreds likely died each week, which kept the four Birkenau crematoria very busy. At full operation, Cremas #2 and #3 could burn around 360 bodies each, per day; Cremas #4 and #5, around 200 per day. And with required down-time, maintenance, cleaning, and repairs, the actual rates were much less. Plus, Crema #4 was damaged early on and operated only for about three months before being permanently shut down.

Thus, with periodic surges of fatalities, many bodies had to be stored temporarily until they could be burned. Hence the "corpse rooms," which indeed held dead bodies, but not from gassing.

88. What about those pictures of smoking piles of bodies at Auschwitz?
In fact, for at least two extended periods of time, the camp could not keep up with the backlog and so the Germans were forced to burn bodies in the open air.

Bodies allegedly burned in the open, Birkenau, ca. 1944

The first period was in late 1942, before the new Birkenau crematoria were built. With only the one, old, Crema #1 in the main camp, the Germans ended up burning thousands in the open air. *If* (a big 'if') we accept the "6 million," then around 170,000 bodies would have been burned in the open air, over about six months; but this would have been virtually impossible, even for the technically-proficient Germans. In reality, more like 25,000 were burned over that time—still a horrible site, and surely a source of many "gassing" and "mass murder" rumors.

The second period was in summer of 1944, with all those new Hungarian Jews. On the standard view, over 400,000 bodies would have been burned in the open during that year, most in just the two-month peak period. On the more realistic revisionist view, around 60,000 would have been burned in the open that year—in addition to some 28,000 in the three functioning crematoria.

89. There are air photos of Auschwitz from 1944 that show the camp from above—what can we tell from these?

We have today 10 photos of Auschwitz taken from passing planes, for the year 1944. Overall, all 10 photos show a calm and peaceful concentration camp without any obvious signs of activity—despite the fact that the Germans were allegedly killing and burning thousands per day. Four of the photos do show, however, a small plume of smoke arising from a far corner of Birkenau; this is fully consistent with the revisionist view that the Germans were burning hundreds of bodies per day in the open air. But it is totally *inconsistent* with the orthodox view in which 5,000 or 10,000 bodies were burned per day, which would have required 10 or 20 large burning pits that would have been clearly visible from above.

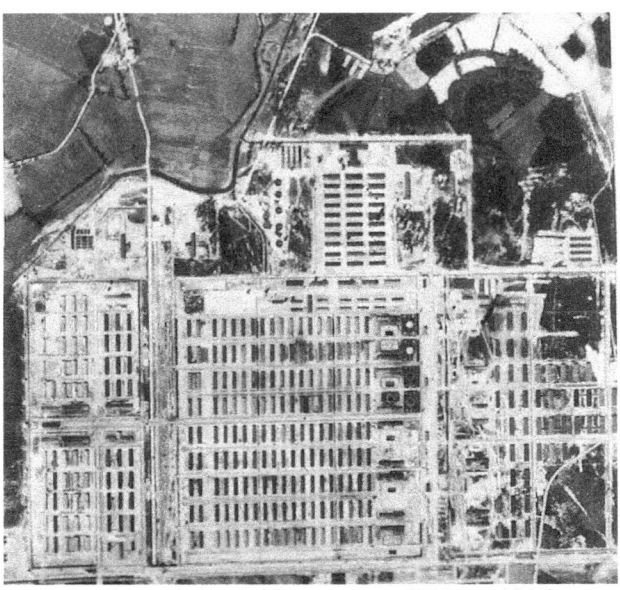

A calm and clear Birkenau camp (31 May 1944)

Once again, of the actual evidence that we have—in this case, 10 air photos—they substantiate the revisionist view of things.

Birkenau camp, with some smoke rising (top, center-right), 23 August 1944

90. Ok, so, no gassings at all at Auschwitz, and lots of deaths from typhus. But still, we have dozens of witnesses who testified to the gassings—what's up with that?

Revisionists have documented at least 130 so-called "eyewitnesses" from Auschwitz, and most have recounted stories of gas chambers. But crucially, none of them ever witnessed a mass gassing. "Of course," says the critic, "all the real witnesses died in the event." Sure—but still, at the end of the day, we have no actual witnesses to the alleged gassing. All we have are people who saw (a) dead bodies (perhaps burning in the open), (b) crematoria running day and night, (c) cans of Zyklon (perhaps), and (d) Jews "disappearing." Everything else was rumor and hearsay.

In addition, these witnesses have included a mixture of fact and fantasy in their statements, such that it can be hard to tell them apart. A good reference source is the new revisionist book, *Holocaust Encyclopedia: Uncensored and Unconstrained* (2023). There, the editors highlight the many witnesses and the many absurd, contradictory, or impossible claims that they made. If a witness says even two or three absurd and obviously false things, then the rest of his or her testimony is thrown into doubt.

91. One of the newest witness books is *Cold Crematorium* by Jozsef Debreczeni, originally written in 1950 but only translated into English in 2023. Is this typical of witness accounts?

Indeed it is, and thus it's worth some elaboration. Debreczeni (real name Jozsef Bruner), described as "an eminent journalist," was a Hungarian Jew deported to Auschwitz for a short time in 1944, when he was 39 years old. As a skilled journalist, one can expect that, first, he is an excellent writer and, second, that he knows how to distinguish fact from fiction. This immediately puts him several steps above the typical witness; and correspondingly, we ought to expect his account to include valuable contributions to our knowledge of the Holocaust, and specifically to Auschwitz and its gas chambers. But not so.

Debreczeni describes his initial capture and movement by train (without dates, unfortunately), and he already knows his ultimate destination: "toward factories of death and gas chambers" (p. 16). Preparing to board the train to Auschwitz, he notes, with resignation: "We're being deported, after all. The best-case scenario: gas chambers. The worst-case: slave labor until death" (p. 22).

As his train approaches the dreaded camp, he recalls, "There were many in our carriage who'd now heard the word ['Auschwitz'] for the first time. A few of us remembered having read about an American film depicting the horrors of the gas chambers" (p. 28). (He must be thinking of those old Movietone newsreels).

In any case, he eventually arrives, and is immediately confronted with a dilemma: "Right or left. To a life of slavery or to death in the gas chamber" (p. 35). This is standard witness confusion; the Germans indeed selected Jews fit for labor from the rest, but the rest were never gassed. "For those on the left, no one saw them ever again." Which he could never know, and regardless, has many possible explanations.

He then embarks on a lengthy discourse about his "first day" in Auschwitz, including a trip to the bathhouse—naturally, since all incoming Jews had to be disinfested of disease-carrying lice. The showers are described in the most horrific terms, as are the barbers who shave off their body hair; "prophylaxis against lice," he rightly notes. A veteran prisoner then approaches him; "you won't wind up in the gas chambers, that's for sure." "See those chimneys there? That's Birkenau. The crematorium city. The smoke there is already—them. Those who stood to the left" (p. 50). This is a classic account: A witness (Debreczeni) hears from another, unnamed prisoner, that the crematorium chimneys—which do not smoke, by the way—were processing dead bodies. But it was of those who died of typhus or other ailments, not those who, moments before, "stood to the left."

"Those chimneys spew that filthy smoke day and night" (no smoke, but they indeed would have been operating fulltime in 1944). The unnamed prisoner then gives another classic, but misguided, account of events:

> Those trucks go straight to Birkenau. It starts the same way as here: in the bathhouse. Everything unfolds with systematic, Teutonic planning. It's in their blood. Panic must be avoided, so to ensure this, a veritable theatrical performance gets underway. Those unfortunates are first made to strip naked. Just like all of you now. They too are shaved and deloused. They think they're going to bathe. Soap is even pressed into their hands. They are pushed through a doorway and, just like everyone else, they find themselves in a shower room. But, instead of hot water, the shower-heads spray gas. That's all there is to it. (p. 51)

A few comments here: (1) Where are the two men, if not already at Birkenau? One cannot see "the chimneys" from the main camp. Someone is confused. (2) If the Jews were given soap, that's because they were heading into a real shower. The Germans would never have given them soap if they were about to be gassed. (3) No expert today claims that the showerheads emitted gas; this is pure propaganda, and utterly false.

Once gassed, says the prisoner, "the bones become glue; human hair is used for mattresses or pillows. There are mountains of children's hair"; but this has now long been debunked as wartime atrocity stories. "I worked in Birkenau," says our prisoner; "[but] not in the inner zone of the crematoriums" (no, of course not…). Then a horrendous statistic: "Three million human bodies have so far gone up in smoke" (p. 52). Again, a ridiculous exaggeration; the actual number, over the entire life of the camp, was at most 1 million, and realistically some 150,000.

Debreczeni closes his Auschwitz day with his own bit of hyperbole:

Birkenau's chimneys spew that filthy brown smoke cease-
lessly above this nightmarish camp of pariahs. Breaks in
operations are unknown in the crematorium city. The toxic
gas has been belching out day and night for years. The furnaces, fired up until they're glowing white, are trembling;
mountains of burning flesh send sooty sparks into the air.
(pp. 56-57)

Again, the chimneys virtually never smoked unless there was a serious
malfunction. Breaks were frequent and regular. The "toxic gas" is a clever
(or misguided) play on words: all exhaust from any chimney is toxic because it includes, in part, carbon monoxide; but this has nothing to do
with the alleged "toxic gas" of the gas chambers. The author seems to
have confused these two notions. Also, he could not know if the ovens
were "glowing white." And there were certainly no "mountains of burning flesh" in the crematoria; at worst, there were small piles of bodies
awaiting incineration. (There could have been piles of bodies being
burned in the open air, but that's not what our author describes.)

In sum, this is an instructive account of the thinking of Jewish inmates, but it is nearly useless as a factual account of an alleged gassing
process.

PART 7

THOUGHTS AND OBSERVATIONS, 80 YEARS LATER

92. Didn't Raul Hilberg admit that Hitler had no budget and no plan for the Holocaust?

Yes. Hilberg died in 2007, but for around four decades he was the leading American scholar of the Holocaust. His book *The Destruction of the European Jews* (1961; 3-volume edition in 2003) was, for years, the definitive work on the subject. Interestingly, Hilberg was able to find only 5.1 million Jewish deaths, but we set that aside for now.

When he was interviewed in 1983, Hilberg had this to say:

> What began in 1941 was a process of destruction not planned in advance, not organized centrally by any agency. There was no blueprint and there was no budget for destructive measures. They were taken step by step, one step at a time…

So he is indeed admitting that there was no budget, no plan, no organizational structure. It was all apparently an *ad hoc*, spontaneous, and arbitrary process. And surely some such killing was like this. But it would have been impossible to organize the deportation, gassing, shooting, and body disposal of 6 million people like this, in just four years or so. If Hilberg is correct on this point—and he surely is—then the death toll was certainly far less than claimed.

93. But Hitler did order the destruction of the Jews, didn't he?

If he did, no one has been able to prove this. In fact, scholars have been looking hard for 80 years now to find a "Hitler order" for the Holocaust; but nothing has been found—not even a passing reference to such an order. One expert, Ian Kershaw, stated with exasperation that, even searching the East European archives in the 1990s, nothing appeared: "Predictably, a written order by Hitler for the 'Final Solution' was not found. The presumption that a single, explicit written order had ever been given had long been dismissed by most historians." As another scholar writes, "when and how the decision was made…has haunted scholars for decades" (Bartov). Despite the utter lack of evidence, it *must* be there, say our Holocaust experts. But it is not.

Lacking evidence of a clear and concise order from Hitler, the scale of the Holocaust was certainly much less than claimed.

94. How did Hilberg explain this situation?

He was so distraught at the lack of an order that he invented a bizarre solution to the problem: "Thus came about not so much a plan being carried out, but an incredible meeting of minds, a consensus mind reading by a far-flung bureaucracy." So Hitler just 'wished' for a Holocaust, and then, by a "consensus mind-reading," it just happened! Like magic!

As Robert Faurisson has said, if it is "incredible," why should we believe it? This clearly shows the desperation of our orthodox scholars.

95. What about those crazy stories of Jews turned into soap, lampshades, and shrunken heads?

More Jewish-inspired nonsense. Soap rumors started circulating in mid-1942, as western Jewish groups tried to shock the world into action against Hitler. In November of that year, the *New York Times* reported on claims by rabbi Stephen Wise, who said that "reliable persons" knew about the Germans "turning Jewish bodies into fats and soap and lubricants" (Nov 26; p. 16). (The same report spoke of killing Jews "by injecting air bubbles into their veins.") Three years later, at the Nuremberg Trials, the Soviets presented actual pieces of soap; as we read in the transcripts: "After cremation, the ashes were used as fertilizer, and in some instances, attempts were made to utilize the fat from the bodies of the victims in the commercial manufacture of soap" (IMT, vol 1, p. 252). Today, all this has been totally discredited; there is not one orthodox historian who accepts that Jews were turned into soap.

The same is true for the lampshades and shrunken-heads stories. After the war, the US military set up a table at Buchenwald camp for local Germans to see, which included, among other things, lamps with leather-like shades and two shrunken heads. The lampshades were also presented as evidence in the trial of the camp commandant's wife, Ilsa Koch. Strangely enough, the lampshades soon disappeared without a trace, as did the heads. Again, today, no one accepts that such things were made from deceased Jews.

96. And what about Anne Frank's diary? Some people call that a hoax.

Her story is only tangentially related to the larger Holocaust narrative, but it is illuminating nonetheless. Anne was in hiding in Amsterdam during the war, and she was, as far as we can tell, shipped to the Bergen-Belsen camp where she died, likely of typhus, in early 1945. Her body was never found.

And this is about all that we know about her. Everything else, including her diary—who wrote it, when, and why—are controversial. The apparently simple matter of a young girl's hand-written diary ends up becoming extremely, and suspiciously, complex. Among the concerns are these: There are at least *three* distinct versions of the diary: (1) her hand-written original, (2) her "rewrite" of her own original, and (3) the "official" version that appeared in print in German and English. There is some overlap, of course, but there are very important differences as well. Also, the contorted story of how Anne's originals were found by a family assistant, stored away for three years, and then returned to her father, Otto. Then we have the character Meyer Levin, a Jewish writer who had a significant but largely cryptic role in the developing of the diary for publication—to the degree that there is a high likelihood that Levin himself wrote the diary and passed it off as Anne's. Finally, there are many bizarre facts about how the family and others allegedly lived in hiding, in an attic, for two full years without being discovered.

The relevance here is that the diary is compulsory reading for thousands, if not millions of children around the world, and it basically serves as pro-Jewish propaganda, building sympathy for the "oppressed Jews" and making our youth susceptible to yet more Holocaust guilt. Even if there is a core of truth to the story, the end product that everyone reads has been so edited, revised, and manipulated that it unquestionably counts as a literary fraud.

97. Some people have suspected for a long time that the Holocaust—the gassings and the "6 million"—were likely false, haven't they?

Yes. The first skeptic was, surprisingly, the top German official Hermann Göring. He was captured after the war and put on trial at Nuremburg. Göring had little to do with the German Jewish policy, but he knew enough to know that the "final solution" to the problem of the Jews was to transport them out of Germany and, ideally, out of Europe altogether. At the trial, he strenuously protested the prosecution's attempts to paint it as mass murder. Shown a film of the piles of bodies at the camps, and told that these were gassing victims (rather than victims of typhus), he purportedly said that the film must be a forgery—which it was. And upon hearing Rudolf Höss testify (under duress) that 2.5 million Jews were gassed at Auschwitz, Göring was aghast; he wrote a private note to Höss, saying "How is it technically possible in the first place to exterminate 2.5 million people within 3½ years?" It was impossible, and Göring knew it.

A few years after the war and the trials, an American academic, John O. Beaty, who had served in US military intelligence during WW2, wrote a fascinating book titled *The Iron Curtain Over America* (1952). There, he addresses the demands on Germany to pay Israel $1.5 billion; as he writes:

> This compensation was said to be for 6,000,000 Jews killed by Hitler. This figure has been used repeatedly, but one who consults statistics and ponders the known facts of recent history cannot do other than wonder how it is arrived at. According to Appendix VII, "Statistics on Religious Affiliation," of *The Immigration and Naturalization Systems of the United States*, the number of Jews in the world is 15,713,638. The *World Almanac*, 1949, p. 289, is cited as the source of the statistical table reproduced on p. 842 of the government document. The article in the *World Almanac* is headed "Religious Population of the World." A corresponding item, with the title, "Population, Worldwide, by Religious Beliefs" is found in the *World Almanac* for 1940 (p. 129), and in it the world Jewish population is given as 15,319,359. If the *World Almanac* figures are correct, the

world's Jewish population did not decrease in the war decade, but showed a small *increase*.

Assuming, however, that the figures of the US document and the *World Almanac* are in error, let us make an examination of the known facts. In the first place, the number of Jews in Germany in 1939 was about 600,000—by some estimates considerably fewer [yes, much fewer]—and of these, many came to the United States, some went to Palestine, and some are still in Germany. As to the Jews in Eastern European lands temporarily overrun by Hitler's troops, the great majority retreated ahead of the German armies into Soviet Russia. Of these, many came later to the US, some moved to Palestine, some unquestionably remained in Soviet Russia and may be a part of the Jewish force on the Iranian frontier, and enough remained in Eastern Europe or have returned from Soviet Russia to form the hard core of the new ruling bureaucracy in satellite countries [of Eastern Europe].

It is hard to see how all these migrations and all these power accomplishments can have come about with a Jewish population much less than that which existed in Eastern Europe before World War II. Thus, the known facts on Jewish migration and Jewish power in Eastern Europe tend …to raise a question as to where Hitler got the 6,000,000 Jews he is said to have killed.

Well said! This is one of the earliest "revisionist" statements by an academic, anywhere, in the years just after the war.

Finally, we have Dr. Charles Larson, a US military medical examiner during the war. He worked with General Patton's troops in Germany and conducted many autopsies from various camps. In a story on him from 1980, we read that "Larson has talked little publicly about the war experience. One reason for his silence has been that his autopsy findings conflicted with the widely-held belief that most Jews in Nazi camps were exterminated by gassing, shooting, or poisoning." Larson said, "What we've heard is that 6 million Jews were exterminated. Part of that is a hoax." The article goes on to explain that "most [Jews] died as a result of the condition to which they were subjected rather than mass exterminations."

"They worked these people to death," said Larson. "In one camp, 90% died of tuberculosis." The article then states, "Larson said that… autopsies showed that death by gassing and shooting were rare. Never was a case of poisoning uncovered, he said." This is a clever way of saying: Larson found not a single "gassing" victim. A "hoax," indeed.

98. After all, the "6 million" is such an astronomically high figure—how could anyone believe it?

Likely because people have no good way to envision a number this large. So we need to put it in more comprehensible terms. Here are three ways to think about it.

First: If the Germans killed 6 million Jews in all, then most of those—about 5.5 million—were killed in just 3½ years: mid-1941 to the end of 1944. So that is 5.5 million killed in 42 months, or an average of 130,000 per month, or *4,365 per day!* Every day! And then they burned or buried that same number, every day—for three and a half years! In the middle of a major war! Who could possibly believe that?

Second: The largest sports stadiums in North America hold about 100,000 people; many of us can therefore envision that number of people. Now, envision *60* such stadiums full of people—that is our "6 million." Now envision that many corpses, somehow disposed of, such that a mere fraction of them were ever found.

Third: Let's say the average Jew was 5 feet tall (Jews are short, after all). If all 6 million bodies were laid end-to-end, they would stretch across 30 million feet, or nearly 5,700 miles—which is roughly the distance from Los Angeles to Paris, France. Impossible!

99.   There are some important postwar memoirs, such as those by Churchill, Eisenhower, and de Gaulle. And there is also one by the leading Jew of that time, Chaim Weizmann—what do those have to add to all this?

Eisenhower's book, *Crusade in Europe* (1948), is a single volume of some 550 pages. Reviewing the index, one finds no listing for either 'Auschwitz,' 'Holocaust,' or 'gas chambers.' The single entry on persecuted Jews refers to the following paragraph:

Of all these displaced persons, the Jews were in the most deplorable condition. For years, they had been beaten, starved, and tortured. Even food, clothes, and decent treatment could not immediately enable them to shake off their hopelessness and apathy. They huddled together—they seemingly derived a feeling of safety out of crowding together in a single room—and there passively awaited whatever might befall. To secure for them adequate shelter, to establish a system of food distribution and medical service, to say nothing of providing decent sanitary facilities, heat, and light was a most difficult task. They were, in many instances, no longer capable of helping themselves; everything had to be done for them. (pp. 439-440)

Surprisingly, no mention by Eisenhower of extermination, mass murder, gassing, crematoria—nothing. Only "beaten, starved, and tortured"— which, given the alternative, isn't so bad.

Dwight D. Eisenhower   Charles de Gaulle

Charles de Gaulle's work, *The Complete War Memoirs* (1954-1959/1964), consists of three volumes and a total of more than 2,000 pages. In the index, we again find no reference whatsoever to 'Auschwitz,' 'Holocaust,' or 'gas chambers'—nor this time even to Jews. This being the latest-written of the three works (the third volume of the original French edition appeared only in 1959), De Gaulle obviously had plenty of time to reflect on the Holocaust; evidently it merited no discussion at all.

The largest memoir was written by Churchill. *The Second World War* (1948-1953) is a massive, six-volume account of the war, consuming nearly 4,500 pages of text. Once again, the indices (one per volume) have no entries at all for 'Auschwitz,' 'Holocaust,' or 'gas chamber.' There are a few references to Jews, but most are simple passing comments. Only one entry, out of six volumes, addresses Jewish persecution. In Volume 1, page 58, we find one single phrase: "brutalities towards the Jews were rampant." (There is one further mention, not in the main text but in the Appendix to Volume 6: In a short note to Anthony Eden, allegedly referring to the Hungarian operation at Auschwitz, Churchill wrote, "There is no doubt that this is probably the greatest and most horrible crime ever committed in the whole history of the world, and it has been done by scientific machinery by nominally civilized men in the name of a great State and one of the leading races of Europe" [p. 693]. Notably, there is no explicit mention of either Auschwitz, gas chambers, or Jews.)

These men all knew what transpired at Nuremberg. They saw the concentration camp photos, and they personally visited some of the sites. They had access to the most confidential information available. And yet, no extermination camps, no '6 million,' no gas chambers, no Auschwitz—only beatings, starvation, and assorted brutalities. It is almost as if they thought there was no Holocaust at all.

But what about leading Jews like Weizmann? Surely he knew what was happening; surely he would have given the world a graphic and detailed exposition on the nature of the Holocaust. As it happens, Weizmann wrote an extended autobiography, *Trial and Error*, in 1947 (published in 1949), running to 500 pages of details on all aspects of the war. And yet, one searches in vain for any reference to Auschwitz, Treblinka, Belzec, or any of the infamous camps; they are invisible here. Mention of the dreaded gas chambers occurs only a single time: "[Some local Polish Jews] perished, with over three million other Polish Jews, in the concentration camps and the gas chambers or in the last desperate uprising of the Warsaw ghetto" (p. 414). But not at Auschwitz or indeed anywhere in particular.

And the "6 million" appears just twice: In a public speech of November 1936, says Weizmann, "I spoke of the six million Jews (a bitter and unconscious prophecy of the number exterminated not long after by

Hitler) pent up in places where they are not wanted" (p. 384). It was just at this time that the Jewish media in the UK and US began to reemphasize, once again, the famous number. It is telling that Weizmann calls this an "unconscious prophecy"—*"How could I have known?"* he is saying to us. The second appearance comes when he recalls a post-war British commission on Palestine: "The British government…refused to accept the view that six million Jews had been done to death in Europe by various scientific mass methods…" (p. 440). What a strange way to describe it! That's all? No elaboration? No details? Nothing more?

So: Four important men, all highly knowledgeable of the entire war situation, possessing vast insider information—and yet virtually nothing on the most tragic mass killing in human history. This is only explicable if the Jewish tragedy was of far less scope than is now portrayed.

100. Some might say, Why is all this important anyway? It was 80 years ago, and everyone involved is dead. What's the big deal?
Why indeed. Under normal circumstances, the deaths of even millions of a given minority amidst a global war would be a matter for historians and specialists alone; the public would rarely or never hear of such a thing, especially nearly a century afterward. But instead, we hear about it *constantly*: in academia, in the news, in politics, in films—everywhere. Who is driving this process? Certainly not the revisionists! They have no power over politics, media, or academia. Obviously it is wealthy and influential Jews who are promoting the conventional Holocaust story, relentlessly, everywhere they can. Obviously they have something to gain from it, as described earlier: power, money, influence, and feelings of guilt.

In the English-speaking world, the facts of Jewish power are so well-documented by now as to be trite. In the US, Jews own or control all the leading media conglomerates: ABC/Disney (Bob Iger, Alan Horn, Peter Rice), Warner Discovery (David Zaslav, David Leavy, Michael De Luca), NBC/Universal (Brian Roberts, David Cohen, Bonnie Hammer), Fox Corp (Lachlan Murdoch—strongly Zionist), and Paramount (Shari Redstone, Bob Bakish, Susan Zirinsky). News, cable television, entertainment, films… all firmly under Jewish control. In American politics, it is no better: the Biden administration is packed with Jews, including Antony Blinken, Alejandro Mayorkas, Janet Yellen, Merrick Garland, Jeff Zients, Mandy Cohen, and many others. And this is not to mention that all of Biden's children married Jews, and that VP Harris is married to a Jew. This is not a coincidence; Jewish money and Jewish influence have led directly to this state of affairs. Jews give at least 25% (Republicans) and at least 50% (Democrats) of all political donation funds. This money buys vast influence at all levels.

The situation is the same, sadly, in Canada, the UK, and Australia. The media and the governments in these nations are comparably affected by their own Jewish lobbies, to such an effect that no contrary ideas, no dissenting opinions, are allowed. And certainly, no uncomfortable truths are allowed to be discussed in public.

And via US and Anglo influence on NATO and the rest of Europe, virtually all Western nations fall into line; there shall be no questioning of the Holocaust, and no doubting of the official storyline.

Even our children and teens are not immune. How many primary- and secondary-school students are compelled each year to read Holocaust stories like *Anne Frank's Diary*, or *Number the Stars*, or *Maus I*, or *Night*, or *The Yellow Star*, or *Milkweed*? How many annual school trips are made to the hundreds of Holocaust museums and memorials around the world? How many lectures, assignments, and papers cover this topic?

The bottom line is this: We are not allowed to forget about the Holocaust, even if we wanted to. Since this is undeniable, we must get our facts straight. We need to get to the truth.

Clearly, then, the orthodox Holocaust story must be *very* important to the Jewish power structure. So important, in fact, that they are willing to fire, fine, or imprison anyone who dares to challenge their story. Consequently, it must lie at the heart of their power; it must be their central tool—a guilt-tool—by which to coerce a gullible and well-meaning public into letting them acquire vast wealth and exert far-ranging power.

All this is self-evidently true. Therefore, getting to the truth of the Holocaust is arguably the single most important task in contemporary Western society. It is indeed "a big deal"—a *very* big deal.

AFTERWORD

Hopefully, this very brief look at the Holocaust has given the reader much food for thought, and on a topic that, at first, seems obscure, but which in reality is of central importance to our modern world. This is intended only as a cursory overview, addressing most of the central points of dispute. Obviously, much more needs to be said, and many important topics were passed over. Here are a few issues that could easily raise many more "questions":

Jewish-instigated genocides preceded Hitler. In 1932, as Hitler's party was closing in on power in Germany, the Jewish leaders in the Soviet Union were busy conducting mass-murders against their own people. A particularly gruesome one was the event known as the Holodomor, which was an intentional famine directed against the Ukraine (because of their strongly nationalist activities). During the two years 1932 to 1933, millions of Ukrainians died; estimates range from 3.5 million to as many as 20 million. This 'holocaust' certainly cost far more lives than Hitler's alleged Holocaust.

Sadly, many Soviet Jews were responsible for this tragedy. Lazar Kaganovitch and Mendel Khatayevich had leading roles, but OGPU director Genrikh Yagoda played a large part, as did non-Jew Vyacheslav Molotov (who was married to a Jewess). Many more Ukrainians and others died in the notorious Gulag system, created by a Jew, Naftaly Frenkel, and run by two more Jews, Lazar Kogon and Matvei Berman. In short, Russians had many reasons to hate Jews, and what's more, the Germans were keenly aware of all this and thus justifiably worried at what the Bolshevik Jews might do to them.

The Wannsee Conference of January 1942 is entirely innocuous. This event, sometimes claimed to be the "formalization" of the Holocaust, in fact discussed only evacuation of Jews to the East, where they would be concentrated and held, safely away from the German Reich; this was the "final solution" to the Jewish Question. Many of these Jews would also be used as forced labor.

But despite the clear and unambiguous wording, Western scholars have insisted that this was all "coded" language, and that "evacuation east was a euphemism for death." One of the attendees, Adolf Eichmann, testified much later that there was informal talk of killing, liquidation, and so on, but this was extracted while he was in Israeli custody in 1960; owing to the circumstances, nothing Eichmann said there can be accepted as trustworthy.

And this is not to mention the fact that we have five or six versions of the meeting minutes, and they all do not agree. Some or all of them have been altered, by unknown persons for unknown reasons. Thus, the "Wannsee protocol" is far from the smoking gun that our orthodox historians would like us to believe.

Before the war, major nations agreed to help Germany remove its Jews. Question 35 addressed the Evian Conference of July 1938, in which 32 nations—including the US, UK, and France—refused to accept any German Jews. But even though they themselves would not take them, they did agree that (a) Germany was within its rights to expel the Jews, and (b) that the 32 nations would help to pay the relocation cost, to some undetermined location.

Then, on 15 February 1939, it was reported in American papers that the participating nations had "provisionally accepted a German plan for removing Jews from Germany." They even authorized the creation of a "settlement corporation" to help pay the estimated cost of $300 million (equivalent to $6.5 billion today). Clearly, the major nations had no problem, at that time, with Hitler's policy of a territorial "final solution." Likely, Zionist Jews supported the relocation, as long as the destination was Palestine (not yet Israel).

Strange how Hitler's plan, later denounced as evil, was initially accepted and even funded by the Western nations.

In retrospect, Hitler clearly had some very good reasons for wanting to remove all the Jews from Germany. As he said way back in his letter of 1919, the Jews had a detrimental influence on society—culturally, morally, and intellectually; this fact had been widely discussed in German society for decades prior to Hitler's letter (see *Classic Essays on the Jewish Question*, T. Dalton, ed., 2022). It was at this same time that the Bolshevik/communist Jews seized power in Russia, and began murdering millions of their own people (as noted above). Then in his *Mein Kampf*, Hitler described his personal experiences with Viennese Jews and their role in criminality, subversion, immorality, and maliciousness.

Hitler rose to power by opposing the Jewish Marxists that ruled in Germany as part of the Weimar government; as they witnessed his growing influence, they began to demonize him and his followers. Hitler's sole 'fault' was wanting a Germany for the Germans, not for the Jews.

When Hitler finally ascended to power in early 1933, the Jews were appalled, and thus very quickly, by March of that year, they declared a kind of global 'war' against him (recall Question 34). This Jewish-led economic boycott threatened Germany's still-fragile economy, compelling Hitler to take increasingly urgent measures against them. When that failed to unseat Hitler, the Jews began to agitate for literal war against him—something which began at least by 1936. Led by British and American Jews, a kind of global coalition against Germany was formed, one which included, incredibly, even the Soviet Union—the very nation that was busy committing monumental crimes against its own people. (And in retrospect, this is understandable, given that western 'capitalist' Jews had a longstanding relationship with the 'communist' Soviet Jews.)

Hitler could see the pressure steadily growing against him, from all sides—and all because he wanted a Germany for the Germans, and because the German people supported him! What was he to do? *Jews, pack up and get out*—that was his message, for years.

But things changed when England and France declared war on him in September 1939; the Jews had initiated an actual war against his nation, and so he did what any other leader would do: he rounded them up, interned them in camps, and began forcible deportations. As the war grew in scope and intensity, the deportees began dying from a variety of causes: illness, disease, malnutrition, and so on. Many of those that actively resisted were executed. Again, this was in line with international norms of the time; only now, because it was *Jews*, did it suddenly become "a Holocaust."

Hitler was not alone; other nations could see what the Jews were doing. Here's one example: in a very brief report in the *New York Times* of 16 August 1941, it was reported that Germany's ally, Japan, was fully aware of the vital Jewish role. "Newspapers today [in Japan] loosed a torrent of abuse against Roosevelt and Churchill for their war aims declaration, charging that it is part of an intensified campaign to encircle Japan and [is] a Jewish plot." We note that this was four months before Pearl Harbor; the US was not, officially, at war yet.

> **Japanese See Jewish Plot**
>
> TOKYO, Saturday, Aug. 16 (U.P) —Newspapers today loosed a torrent of abuse against President Roosevelt and Prime Minister Churchill for their war aims declaration, charging that it is part of an intensified campaign to encircle Japan and a Jewish plot.
>
> The weekly magazine of the newspaper Asahi said that the President and Mr. Churchill were backed by "Jewish influence and power."
>
> "Jews re-elected Roosevelt for a third term," it said. "Jews coaxed Churchill to war against Germany. Jews are also backing Stalin. Jews are conspiring to overthrow the world-ruling powers.
>
> "Jews want bases in the Atlantic and Pacific, at Burma, and oases in China from which to bomb Japan. Jews have abandoned mere cultural domination ambitions and are now seeking to encircle countries which are trying to establish a new order. These remarks may be laughed off as the dream of a fiction writer but they are most important."

A prominent periodical, *Asahi*, stated that Roosevelt and Churchill "were backed by 'Jewish influence and power'." "Jews coaxed Churchill to war against Germany. Jews are also backing Stalin. Jews are conspiring to overthrow the world-ruling powers," the story adds. "Jews…are trying to establish a new [global] order," says *Asahi*.

Granted that, since Japan was allied with Germany, they would naturally be sympathetic to German views. But still, it is a remarkable set of claims; and they were surely more extensive and more detailed than the embarrassed NYT wanted to admit.

Surviving German leaders have repudiated the conventional view. Some might say this is obvious, but in reality, many Germans who survived the war and the postwar trials were bullied, bribed, or coerced into making damning statements, or into saying nothing at all. But not everyone. One example is Major General Otto Remer. Just 20 years old when Hitler took power, he rose to battalion commander in 1943, leading troops on the Eastern Front. In July 1944, he was decisive in putting down an attempted coup against Hitler, and in early 1945 was promoted to general. After the war, he was captured, imprisoned, and then released in 1947.

Unlike many other former "Nazis," Remer was unrepentant. Although he had no role in the Jewish Question and had not visited any of the camps, he had clear opinions on the matter, based on his direct contact with the highest levels of Hitler's government. In a 1987 interview, he said:

> I want to be clear with you. Jews and others were put into many camps from 1933 to 1945, and at the end of the war,

many ended up dying in these camps. However, there was no German policy to purposely kill these inmates based on their race or religion. The story goes that we hated them so much, since they were so successful and we were jealous of them, that we rounded them up and when we couldn't get them out of Europe, we gassed them. I saw the movies the Allies made us watch, I heard the stories they would freely tell on the radio, and read the books they write. ...

I say, use your thinking cap, examine the testimonies with an open mind; ask yourself *if it is possible*. Some Jews were put into camps, yes, just as Japanese were put into camps in America—because they were viewed as a threat. We viewed the Jewish problem as being very serious; they assassinated many of our diplomats; their newspapers encouraged disobedience; and we reacted against them. For every action, there is a reaction. When war started, more were rounded up and sent to camps, to be moved east, from where they came. We used them for very important labor... So why kill people who could help create what you need?

I understand that fingers are pointed at us; just the very fact we had people, even whole families, in camps looks bad. However, to say they were targeted for murder ups the ante of pure evil. While I was never in a camp, I did see some of the inmates after the war, and never heard anything of a plan to kill them. We executed orders very well, so I assure you if there had been an order to kill them all, there would be none left in Europe. Instead, there are millions of survivors.

We would not have used an insecticide to do it either; Zyklon-B was a fumigant that all nations used to kill lice, which cause typhus, which killed millions after the first war [WW1]. The American [equivalent was] DDT, so the Jews expect us to believe DDT was used to gas them, while we see newsreels of GI's and Wehrmacht soldiers getting sprayed with it before going on leave.

The many photos of dead bodies that the Allies paraded around that purport to show proof, are in truth, evidence of why delousing was needed. The Allies destroyed rail lines, bridges, roads, and airports so that no supplies could get to German cities or the camps. One sad example of the Allies killing inmates is the train found at Dachau; it was bringing inmates to the camp from the east, and fighters attacked it. Dozens died instantly from the attack, and the guards fled, leaving dozens more wounded to die. The allied press had a happy time showing a "Nazi" atrocity. …

The prisoners got sick, withered away, and died, many times right when the Allies entered the camps. Many died even while under allied care; it took weeks to stop the outbreaks, and thousands of prisoners died. The Allies caused these deaths, although not intentionally. It was just easy to blame a policy of extermination instead of telling the truth.

The only area that the Jews have open to them is the killings of partisans, many of whom were Jewish. If they fought against us as non-combatants, they ended up executed as common criminals. I saw this in person when a band was caught trying to blow up a rail bridge: they were tried and hung, as any nation would have done. It had nothing to do with who they were; it was their actions that sealed their fate to the rope.

All this accords with the revisionist view, and largely exonerates Hitler and others from charges of genocide. Of course, this is hardly proof; but still, Remer was at risk in saying such things; as an "ex-Nazi," he had a permanent target on his back and it would have been much easier to say nothing. Instead, he openly and publicly offered up some very comfortable views. (Remer died peacefully in Spain in 1997.)

Jews truly do seem to dislike non-Jews, even hate them. Obviously there are exceptions but, by and large, powerful and influential Jews do seem to pursue actions and policies that are intrinsically harmful to non-Jews. This has been observed for literally thousands of years: Back in 300 BC, Greek historian Hecateus of Abdera remarked that Moses and his people "introduced a way of life which was, to a certain extent, misanthropic and hostile to foreigners." This viewpoint was then confirmed by dozens of scholars and academics over the centuries—for details, see the book *Eternal Strangers* (T. Dalton, 2020). This is no coincidence and it is not mindless anti-Semitism; Jews truly do hate others, seek to dominate them, and seek to do them harm if they can profit thereby.

This is no mere speculation; it is well-documented in the Old Testament, in the Talmud, and in the Shulchan Aruch. Initially a kind of survival strategy in the harsh Middle Eastern desert, such attitudes became codified in the Jewish religion and in their social and moral codes. Today, after thousands of years, it has become ingrained in the Jewish soul, as a kind of genetic disposition to be hostile, suspicious, and exploitative. Non-Jews who fail to understand this are at great peril.

Lest anyone doubt this today, one need only observe the current (2024-2025) actions by Israel in Gaza, Lebanon, and beyond. The Israeli government, with virtually the full backing of their people (at home and abroad), are conducting a true genocide, a real holocaust, on the Palestinian people. With an official death toll exceeding 40,000—and likely double or triple this figure—Israeli Jews have proven themselves to be brutal killers of innocent men, women, and children. And they do so in the open, televised, for all the world to see. And they do not care.

How is this possible? How can it be that the world rallied together, at great expense, to crush Hitler but now cannot life a finger (apart from Iran and its proxies) to crush the Jews? We know why: The United States, which is the supreme military power on Earth and holder of a UN veto, can block any action against the Jewish state even as it continues to supply weapons and funds. And it does this because the US government is largely under control of the Jewish Lobby—thanks to their millions in campaign donations and potent threats against any dissenters.

As for moral justification, Jews will invoke the Holocaust: "never again," they say, must an enemy of the Jews—here, militant Palestinians and Muslims—pose a mortal threat; therefore, any action, no matter how brutal or how extreme, is permissible. Any White Europeans—the very people who allegedly carried out the "Nazi Holocaust"—that oppose this genocide are tarred as anti-Semites, Jew-haters, or Holocaust-deniers, and consequently suffer all the negative effects of this branding. It a circular and malevolent logic, but it largely works because too few White Europeans are willing to work together to combat this Hebraic maliciousness;

and they are unwilling to pay the price for victory. As a result, all the world suffers under Jewish dominion.

If we want to change this situation, then we need to address the root of the Jewish power structure and the central "guilt-tool" that they deploy against White European people: the Holocaust. This booklet can be one small step in that direction.

NOTES AND REFERENCES
TO SELECTED QUESTIONS

Question 5: For works by several of these individuals, see the Bibliography.

Question 6: See *Debating the Holocaust* (2020, T. Dalton), pp. 297-301.

Question 8: See *Eternal Strangers* (2020, T. Dalton) and *Classic Essays on the Jewish Question: 1850 to 1945* (2022, T. Dalton).

Question 13: See *Debating the Holocaust*, pp. 55-64. See also *The First Holocaust* (2024, D. Heddesheimer).

Question 15: Same as above.

Question 17: Same as above.

Question 19: See *Mein Kampf*, vol 1 (2022; T. Dalton, trans.), chapter 2, pp. 57-98. On the Voltaire quote, see *Eternal Strangers*, p. 72.

Question 20: See *The Jewish Hand in the World Wars* (2019, T. Dalton). For the Ford quote, see his *The International Jew*, vol 2 (2024, T. Dalton, ed.), p. 106—chapter 56, dated 11 June 1921.

Question 21: See *The Jewish Hand*, pp. 60-64.

Question 22: See *The Jewish Hand*, pp. 56-59.

Question 23: See *The Jewish Hand*, pp. 79-89.

Question 24: See *Mein Kampf*, vol 1, chapter 2, pp. 219-220.

Question 25: See *Hitler on the Jews* (2024), pp. 135-137. Also reproduced in *Classic Essays on the Jewish Question*, pp. 211-214.

Question 26: See *Mein Kampf*, vol 2, chapter 15, p. 310. See also *Hitler on the Jews*, p. 238.

Question 27: See *The Jewish Hand*, pp. 85-89.

Question 28: On the Bryant quote, see his *Unfinished Victory* (1940), pp. 142-145.

Question 30: See *The Jewish Hand*, pp. 95-107.

Question 31: See *Churchill and the Jews*, by Martin Gilbert (2008), p. 4.

Question 34: For the corresponding quotes, see Vydra (2017), p. 212; Ginsberg (2013), p. 40; Cowling (1975), p. 288. See also the excellent discussion in Jones (2024).

Question 37: See *The Jewish Hand*, p. 110.

Question 38: See *The Jewish Hand*, p. 121.

Question 40: See *Goebbels on the Jews: The Complete Diary Entries* (2024; T. Dalton, ed.). On the Madagascar Plan, see the entry "Madagascar" in *The Holocaust Encyclopedia: Uncensored and Unconstrained* (2023).

Question 44: See *Debating the Holocaust*, pp. 76-81.

Question 68: See *Debating the Holocaust*, p. 79.

Question 69: See *Debating the Holocaust*, p. 259.

Question 70: For a brief discussion, see *Debating*, pp. 114-127. For a more detailed examination, see *The Gas Vans* (2023; S. Alvarez).

Question 75: See *Debating the Holocaust*, pp. 122-125.

Question 77: See: *The "Operation Reinhardt" Camps Treblinka, Sobibór, Bełżec* (2021; C. Mattogno); *Belzec* (2016; C. Mattogno); *Treblinka* (2020; C. Mattogno and J. Graf); *Sobibor* (2020; J. Graf, T. Kues, C. Mattogno).

Question 81: *Concentration Camp Majdanek* (2016; J. Graf and C. Mattogno).

Question 89: See *Debating the Holocaust*, pp. 234-243. See also Air-Photo Evidence (2020; Armreg).

Question 90: For an excellent summary of all the relevant witnesses, see the *Holocaust Encyclopedia* (2023; Armreg).

Question 91: *Cold Crematorium: Reporting from the Land of Auschwitz* (1950 /2023), by József Debreczeni.

Question 92: *New York Newsday*, 23 February 1983, Part II, p. 3.

Question 93: Kershaw (2008), p. 96; Bartov (2015), p. 7.

Question 97: On the Larson story, see "Concentration Camp Conditions Killed Most Inmates, Doctor Says"; *The Wichita Eagle*, 1 April 1980, p. 4C.

Bibliography

Alvarez, S. 2023. *The Gas Vans*. Castle Hill.

Armreg. 2024. *Holocaust Encyclopedia: Uncensored and Unconstrained*. Online: <https://nukebook.org>

Bartov, O. 2015. *The Holocaust*. Routledge.

Beaumont, J. 2023. *The Truth Will Set You Free: The Case for Holocaust Revisionism*. Fidelity.

Beaty, J. 1951. *The Iron Curtain Over America*. Wilkinson.

Berg, F. 1986. "Zyklon B and the German delousing chambers." *Journal of Historical Review*, 7(1): 73-94.

Berg, F. 1988. "Typhus and the Jews." *Journal of Historical Review*, 8(4): 433-481.

Berg, F. 2003. "Poison gas *über alles*." *The Revisionist*, 1(1): 37-47.

Berg, F. 2008. "Nazi railroad delousing tunnels for public health, or mass murder?" Online: <http://www.nazigassings.com/railroad.html>

Berg, F. 2019. "Diesel gas chambers: Ideal for torture—absurd for murder," in Rudolf (2019: 431-473).

Bryant, A. 1940. *Unfinished Victory*. Macmillan.

Butz, A. 2000. "On the 1944 deportations of Hungarian Jews." *Journal of Historical Review*, 19(4): 19-28.

Butz, A. 2000. "The greatest dirty open secret." *Journal of Historical Review*, 19(5): 18-21.

Butz, A. 2015. *The Hoax of the Twentieth Century*. (4th ed.) Castle Hill.

Churchill, W. 1948-1953. *The Second World War*. Cassell.

Cowling, M. 1975. *The Impact of Hitler*. Cambridge University Press.

Crowell, S. 2000. "Bomb shelters in Birkenau: A reappraisal." Online: <http://codoh.com/library/document/904/>

Crowell, S. 2001. "The basement showers of crematorium III." *Journal of Historical Review*, 20(2): 17-20.

Crowell, S. 2001. "Beyond Auschwitz." *Journal of Historical Review*, 20(2): 26-35.

Crowell, S. 2011. *The Gas Chamber of Sherlock Holmes*. Nine-banded Books.

Dalton, T. 2011. "Reexamining the 'gas chamber' of Dachau." *Inconvenient History* 3(4).

Dalton, T. 2016. *The Holocaust: An Introduction*. Castle Hill.

Dalton, T. 2019. *The Jewish Hand in the World Wars*. Castle Hill.

Dalton, T. 2020. *Debating the Holocaust: A New Look at Both Sides* (4th ed.). Castle Hill.

Dalton, T. 2020. *Eternal Strangers: Critical Views of Jews and Judaism Through the Ages*. Castle Hill.

Dalton, T. (ed.). 2022. *Classic Essays on the Jewish Question*. Clemens & Blair.

Dalton, T. (ed.) 2024. *Goebbels on the Jews*. Clemens & Blair.

Debreczeni, J. 1950/2023. *Cold Crematorium*. St. Martin's.

De Gaulle, C. 1954-1959/1964. *The Complete War Memoirs*. Simon and Schuster.

Eisenhower, D. 1948. *Crusade in Europe*. William Heinemann.

Evans, R. 2001. *Lying About Hitler*. Basic Books. (Republished as *Telling Lies About Hitler*, 2002).

Faurisson, R. 1999-2018. *Ecrits Révisionnistes (1974–2018)*. 9 volumes. Edition privée hors-commerce/La Sfinge. Four volumes online: <https://archive.org/details/EcritsRevisionnistes>

Faurisson, R. 2001. "Shoah: Fictive images and mere belief?" *Journal of Historical Review*, 20(1): 6.

Faurisson, R. 2002. "My revisionist method." *Journal of Historical Review*, 21(2): 7-14.

Faurisson, R. 2003. "How many deaths at Auschwitz?" *The Revisionist*, 1(1): 17-23.

Faurisson, R. 2004. "Treblinka: An exceptional guide." *The Revisionist*, 2(1): 78-82.

Faurisson, R. 2019. "Witnesses to the gas chambers of Auschwitz," in Rudolf (2019: 129-139).

Ford, H. 2024. *The International Jew: The Definitive Edition* (2 volumes; T. Dalton, ed.). Clemens & Blair.

Gilbert, M. 2008. *Churchill and the Jews*. Henry Holt.

Ginsberg, B. 2013. *How the Jews Defeated Hitler*. Rowman & Littlefield.

Graf, J. 2000. "What happened to the Jews who were deported to Auschwitz but were not registered there?" *Journal of Historical Review*, 19(4): 4-18.

Graf, J. 2015. *The Giant with Feet of Clay* (2nd ed.). Castle Hill.

Graf, J. 2019. *Auschwitz: Eyewitness Reports and Perpetrator Confessions of the Holocaust*. Castle Hill.

Graf, J. and Mattogno, C. 2016. *Concentration Camp Majdanek* (3rd ed.). Castle Hill.

Graf, J., Kues, T., and Mattogno, C. 2020. *Sobibór: Holocaust Propaganda and Reality*. Castle Hill.

Heddesheimer, D. 2018. *The First Holocaust* (5th ed.). Castle Hill.

Hilberg, R. 1961/2003. *The Destruction of the European Jews*. Yale University Press.

Hitler, A. 2000. *Table Talk*. Enigma.

Hitler, A. 2022. *Mein Kampf* (2 volumes; T. Dalton, trans.). Clemens & Blair.

Hitler, A. 2024. *Hitler on the Jews* (T. Dalton, ed.). Clemens & Blair.

Hoffmann, M. 1985. *The Great Holocaust Trial*. IHR.

Jones, M. 2024. "A conflict of philosophies." Online: <www.unz.com>

Kershaw, I. 2008. *Hitler, the Germans, and the Final Solution*. Yale University Press.

Kollerstrom, N. 2023. *Breaking the Spell*. Castle Hill.

Kues, T. 2010. "Chil Rajchman's Treblinka memoirs." *Inconvenient History* 2(1).

Leuchter, F. *et al.* 2017. *The Leuchter Reports* (5th ed.). Castle Hill.

Lipstadt, D. 2010. "Denial," in Hayes and Roth (eds.), *Oxford Handbook of Holocaust Studies*. Oxford University Press.

Lough, D. 2015. *No More Champagne: Churchill and His Money*. Picador.

Mattogno, C. 2003. "Auschwitz: Fritjof Meyer's New Revisions." *The Revisionist*, 1(1): 30-37.

Mattogno, C. 2003. "The four million figure of Auschwitz." *The Revisionist*, 1(4): 387-399.

Mattogno, C. 2004. "Combustion experiments with flesh and animal fat." *The Revisionist*, 2(1): 64-72.

Mattogno, C. 2004. "Flames and smoke from the chimneys of crematoria." *The Revisionist*, 2(1): 73-78.

Mattogno, C. 2004. "The 'gas testers' of Auschwitz." *The Revisionist*, 2(2): 140-155.

Mattogno, C. 2004. "The morgues of the crematoria at Birkenau in the light of documents." *The Revisionist*, 2(3): 271-294.

Mattogno, C. 2011. *Bełżec: In Propaganda, Testimonies, Archeological Research, and History*. Barnes Review.

Mattogno, C. 2015. "Patrick Desbois and the 'Mass Graves' of Jews in Ukraine," *Inconvenient History*, 7(3).

Mattogno, C. 2016. "Auschwitz: The End of a Legend," in Rudolf (ed., 2016: 131-212).

Mattogno, C. 2016. *Healthcare in Auschwitz: Medical Care and Special Treatment of Registered Inmates*. Castle Hill.

Mattogno, C. 2016. *Debunking the Bunkers of Auschwitz* (2nd ed). Castle Hill.

Mattogno, C. 2016. *Special Treatment in Auschwitz* (2nc ed). Castle Hill.

Mattogno, C. 2016. *Auschwitz: Crematorium I* (2nd ed). Castle Hill.

Mattogno, C. 2016. *Auschwitz: The First Gassing* (3rd ed.). Castle Hill.

Mattogno, C. 2016. *Inside the Gas Chambers* (2nd ed). Castle Hill.

Mattogno, C. 2016. *Auschwitz: Open Air Incinerations* (2nd ed). Castle Hill.

Mattogno, C. 2017. "The elusive holes of death," in Rudolf and Mattogno (2017: 291-407).

Mattogno, C. 2017. *Chełmno: A German Camp in History and Propaganda* (2nd ed). Castle Hill.

Mattogno, C. 2018. *Auschwitz: A Three-Quarter Century of Propaganda*. Castle Hill.

Mattogno, C. 2019. *The Real Case for Auschwitz* (3rd ed.), Castle Hill.

Mattogno, C. 2020. *Curated Lies: The Auschwitz Museum's Misrepresentations, Distortions and Deceptions*. Castle Hill.

Mattogno, C. 2020. *Commandant of Auschwitz: Rudolf Höss, His Torture and His Forced Confessions*. Castle Hill

Mattogno, C. 2021. *The Cremation Furnaces of Auschwitz*. Castle Hill.

Mattogno, C. 2021. *The "Operation Reinhardt" Camps Treblinka, Sobibór, Bełżec*. Castle Hill.

Mattogno, C. 2022. *The Einsatzgruppen in the Occupied Eastern Territories.* Castle Hill.

Mattogno, C. and Graf, J. 2023. *Treblinka: Extermination Camp or Transit Camp?* (2nd ed.), Castle Hill.

Mattogno, C., Kues, T., and Graf, J. 2015. *The "Extermination Camps" of "Aktion Reinhardt."* Castle Hill.

Mattogno, C. and Nyiszli, M. 2018. *An Auschwitz Doctor's Eyewitness Account.* Castle Hill.

Rassinier, P. 1978. *Debunking the Genocide Myth.* Noontide Press.

Rassinier, P. 1979. *The Real Eichmann Trial.* Historical Review Press.

Rassinier, P. 2022. *Ulysses's Lie.* (2nd ed.) Castle Hill.

Rudolf, G. 2001. "A brief history of forensic examinations of Auschwitz." *Journal of Historical Review*, 20(2): 3-16.

Rudolf, G. 2003. "Cautious mainstream revisionism." *The Revisionist*, 1(1): 23-30.

Rudolf, G. 2004. "On the progress and propagation of Holocaust revisionism." *The Revisionist*, 2(3): 243-249.

Rudolf, G. (ed.) 2016. *Auschwitz: Plain Facts* (2nd ed.). Castle Hill.

Rudolf, G. (ed.) 2019. *Dissecting the Holocaust* (3rd ed.). Castle Hill.

Rudolf, G. 2019. *Auschwitz: Technique and Operation of the Gas Chambers.* Castle Hill.

Rudolf, G. 2020. *The Chemistry of Auschwitz.* Castle Hill.

Rudolf. G. (ed.) 2020. *Air-Photo Evidence* (5th ed.). Castle Hill.

Rudolf, G. and Mattogno, C. 2017. *Auschwitz Lies* (4th ed.). Castle Hill.

Stäglich, W. 1986/2015. *The Auschwitz Myth.* Castle Hill.

Suzuki, I. 2022. *Unmasking Anne Frank: Her Famous Diary Exposed as a Literary Fraud.* Clemens & Blair.

Vydra, Z. 2017. "British Jewry and the attempted boycott of Nazi Germany, 1933-1939," *Theatrum historiae* 21.

Walendy, U. 2019. "Do photographs prove the NS extermination of the Jews?" in Rudolf (2019: 235-261).

Weizmann, C. 1947/1949. *Trial and Error.* Harper.

Wilton, R. 1920/1993. *The Last Days of the Romanovs.* Noontide.

Suggested Websites:

www.unz.com (a variety of good articles on the Holocaust)
www.nukebook.org (online revisionist *Holocaust Encyclopedia*)
www.holocausthandbooks.com (top-rated research books)
www.clemensandblair.com (retailer of high-quality Holocaust books)
www.armreg.co.uk (retailer of high-quality Holocaust books)
www.codoh.com (general information on revisionism)
www.codohforum.com (forum for information and debate on the Holocaust)

INDEX